D o o r

W i d e

O p e n

VIKING
75 years

Jack Kerouac and Joyce Johnson

WITH AN

INTRODUCTION AND

COMMENTARY BY

JOYCE JOHNSON

Door

Wide

Open

A Beat Love Affair in Letters, 1957–1958

VIKING

VIKING
Published by the Penguin Group
Penguin Putnam Inc., 375 Hudson Street,
New York, New York 10014, U.S.A.
Penguin Books Ltd, 27 Wrights Lane,
London W8 5TZ, England
Penguin Books Australia Ltd, Ringwood,
Victoria, Australia
Penguin Books Canada Ltd, 10 Alcorn Avenue,
Toronto, Ontario, Canada M4V 3B2
Penguin Books (N.Z.) Ltd, 182–190 Wairau Road,
Auckland 10, New Zealand

Penguin Books Ltd, Registered Offices:
Harmondsworth, Middlesex, England

First published in 2000 by Viking Penguin,
a member of Penguin Putnam Inc.

1   3   5   7   9   10   8   6   4   2

LIBRARY OF CONGRESS CATALOGING IN PUBLICATION DATA

Kerouac, Jack, 1922–1969.
Door wide open : a beat love affair in letters, 1957–1958 / Jack Kerouac and
Joyce Johnson ; with introduction and commentary by Joyce Johnson.
p.   cm.
ISBN 0-670-89040-5
1. Kerouac, Jack, 1922–1969—Correspondence.   2. Johnson, Joyce,
1935—Correspondence.   3. Authors, American—20th century—Correspondence.
4. Beat generation.   5. Love-letters.   I. Johnson, Joyce, 1935–   . II. Title.
PS3521.E735 Z485 2000
813'.54—dc21   99-053219
[B]

This book is printed on acid-free paper.
∞

Printed in the United States of America
Set in Goudy
Designed by Kathryn Parise

for my breast shaken with doves,

for my derelict dying, with a single mistaken bypasser.

—Federico García Lorca

Acknowledgments

I am deeply grateful to John Sampas for restoring to me an important piece of my past and for suggesting that there was a book in the letters Jack Kerouac and I wrote each other.

Thanks also to my astute Viking editor Paul Slovak, my indefatigable literary agent Irene Skolnick, and to Sterling Lord, whom I first met in September 1957 and who still represents Jack Kerouac.

I must also thank Dorothy Sucher for unearthing the lost letter I wrote her in 1958.

Introduction

Joyce Johnson

Nineteen fifty-seven began with a party. It was down in the Village, on Grove Street. I remember a high-ceilinged white room, a whitewashed brick fireplace, a looming carbon stain behind flaming twists of newspaper. Shouts came up from the street at midnight. I'd gone there with Allen Ginsberg and my best friend Elise Cowen, whom the host, Lucien Carr, kept wickedly calling Eclipse. I felt shy at this party, embarrassed in this older crowd by being only twenty-one. I stared at the black stain in the fireplace and listened in on conversations, turning my glass in my hand. What I remember most of all was the almost palpable presence of an absent guest—a wandering writer with an illogical but musical name, who was said to have written an entire novel in three weeks on a scroll of paper. Everyone spoke of this Kerouac, but I had missed him. He had already streaked through New York and gone, worn out a passionate love affair in a month. A woman several years older than I was named Helen Weaver, whom everyone considered "great," had completely fallen for him, but now she was asking her psychoanalyst what to do. "Jack's too much for her," someone said knowingly. What could that "too much" be? I wondered.

I had seen two pictures of Jack Kerouac. One was on the jacket of a book I stole from the MCA Literary Agency, where I worked as a secretary. Kerouac had briefly been one of their clients—"difficult" was the way people there remembered him, and the stuff he wrote was unsalable—Good-bye to him and good riddance. They deserved whatever trouble Kerouac had given them, I thought. I hated MCA, with its petty intrigues, hated the agent who asked me to wash out her dirty coffee mugs in the ladies' room sink and the pretentious wood-paneled offices decorated with leatherbound "classics"; I had taken one of these off a shelf and found a cardboard box inside the fancy binding.

In the photo on *The Town and the City*, the only novel Kerouac had published so far, he did not look difficult at all. He looked tender, half melancholy, half proud, dressed like an impoverished young college instructor in a dark jacket with a rumpled collar, a white shirt, and a tightly knotted obligatory necktie. In the second photo, taken seven years later for an article on the San Francisco Renaissance published in the September 1956 issue of *Mademoiselle*, I caught a glimpse of the Kerouac who could be "too much." The necktie was gone, replaced by a crucifix in the open neck of a checked shirt. The man in this photo had strands of wet black hair plastered against his forehead; he looked as if he were passing through fire.

I wanted to meet him, even though the thought of it scared me a little. In those days I tended to go toward what scared me. My latest philosophy of life had become "Nothing to lose, try anything." A boy I'd known at college had recently told me, "You remind me of a doll that's been taken out of the window and put out on the street." I wrote down this observation because I thought it worth recording. Next to it I added, "Probably true?"

Three weeks after the party I was visiting Elise's apartment in Yorkville, where Allen Ginsberg and his lover Peter Orlovsky were staying, when the phone rang. Allen said, "There's someone who wants to speak to you." It was Kerouac in a phone booth on Eighth Street, back in town after a visit to his mother in Florida; Helen Weaver's psychoanalyst had finally advised her to kick him out, and he was staying in a depressing hotel on Eighth Street.

The voice at the other end of the line was surprisingly diffident. Allen Ginsberg had told him I was "nice," and he'd like to meet me—right away, in fact. If I'd come right down to Howard Johnson's in the Village, he'd be waiting for me at the lunch counter in a red-and-black-checked flannel shirt.

Forty years later, after Ginsberg's sudden death, I found myself wondering what had prompted him to arrange this fateful blind date. My friendship with Allen went all the way back to when I met him at sixteen at an apartment near Columbia where I had no business being; but I had never asked him this question. I decided that a characteristic Ginsbergian mixture of kindliness, practicality, and erotic mischief had probably been at work. Allen was always taking care of people, looking out for his friends. Nine months before the publication of *On the Road*, Jack was womanless and dead broke. I was a girl with a reasonably hip outlook, who must have seemed at loose ends, with no current steady boyfriend, and—an important consideration from Allen's point of view—I had an apartment. Whatever ultimately happened between Jack and this girl Joyce, maybe they'd dig each other for a while, have some interesting, illuminating moments.

With no second thoughts, I rushed downtown to meet Kerouac, who—no longer in black and white—was one of the most compelling-looking men I'd ever seen with his black hair, blue eyes, and ruddy complexion. After an hour or so of conversation, when Jack asked whether he could come home with me, I answered with deceptive coolness, "If you wish." Young women were not supposed to have such adventures in 1957.

Back then my name was still Joyce Glassman. "Glassgirl," my friend Elise Cowen would affectionately call me, an ironic reminder of the sheltered life I'd been forced to lead until fairly recently, the feeling I used to have of looking out at the world from behind a sheet of glass while other people had intense, significant collisions with reality. Glass was a recurring image in the novel I had begun to write, about a girl like me in her last week at a New York women's college that strongly resembled my alma mater, Barnard. My tentative title for this book was *The Green Wall*, but I played with the idea of calling it *Breaking Windows*.

I seemed to be having great difficulty writing this novel. Words came slowly and painfully, and the next day I'd hate what I'd written and start all over again. Very shyly I confessed to Kerouac that I was a writer, too. He immediately advised me never to revise, the first thought was always best, which was not a dictum I was ever able to follow. I didn't tell him I had some fear of my intended subject matter. My novel was not going to be one that most people would approve of or that I would want my innocent parents to read. I was going to be unsparingly truthful. Having read Gide and Dostoyevsky, I'd become fascinated by the gratuitous act. My heroine would *decide* to lose her burdensome virginity—not out of passion but in an attempt to satisfy her curiosity, to have something real happen to her. The problem with writing about sexual matters, if you were a young woman back then, was that everyone would then draw the conclusion that you had firsthand knowledge of the subject. In *Bonjour Tristesse* Françoise Sagan had shocked everyone and gotten away with it, but she was French.

Even men, in the 1950s, could not write about the full range of human experience without being penalized. These were the days when copies of Henry Miller's novels and the unexpurgated *Lady Chatterley's Lover* had to be smuggled in from abroad. One reason Kerouac was practically destitute at the time I met him was that since 1950 no one had dared to publish his books. *On the Road*— its final draft written in one extraordinary burst of creative energy—had sat in the offices of Viking Press for three bitter years, and it was not until January 1957 that the hesitant publisher felt the climate was right to give Jack a contract for it. Four decades later, when the first volume of Kerouac's *Selected Letters* was published, I was struck by Jack's poignant plea to his Viking editors* in 1955. With the fate of *On the Road* still hanging fire, he asked them for a stipend of $25 a month, which would enable him to live

*Malcolm Cowley, well known for his critical studies of the Lost Generation writers, was an emeritus advisory editor at Viking Press; his associate Keith Jennison would later oversee the publication of *On the Road*.

in a hut in Mexico and go on writing. His request was so outrageously modest it was evidently not taken seriously. "Cowley laughed," Jack reported to Ginsberg, "and Jennison was with him and they said, 'You certainly aren't holding us up, boy.'"

By the mid-1960s the culture had changed so much and so quickly that it is hard today for ahistorical young people to remember that there were transitional years before certain kinds of freedom we now take for granted could be fully achieved. The Beats—now routinely castigated by doctrinaire feminists for their macho behavior and attitudes—ushered in sexual liberation, which would not only bring a new and permanent openness to American art and literature but transform life for everyone. My story may seem unique because circumstances brought Kerouac and me together at a crucial moment. But in the bland and sinister 1950s there were thousands like me—women as well as men—young people with longings we couldn't yet articulate bottled up inside us. Ginsberg and Kerouac would give powerful, irresistible voices to these subversive longings; they'd release us from our weirdness, our isolation, tell us we were not alone.

My upbringing, in some important respects, had been quite different from the way most girls were raised in the 1940s and '50s. Yet in an inverse way the essential messages were the same. I had grown up with the unconventional idea that I would have to make my own way in the world, that I could not be dependent upon any man. When I was thirteen, my mother had revealed to me how disappointed she was in her marriage to my gentle, unsuccessful father, a betrayal I couldn't forgive her for. My mother was an ambitious, frustrated, terrified woman, warped by the bitterness of ending up a mere housewife, making ends meet on $25 a week while struggling to maintain a genteel facade. When I was born, her brother wrote her, "At last you have something of your own!" My mother needed to believe that she had produced a prodigy; her worst fear was that I would leave her. In her youth she had wanted to become a concert singer, so she convinced herself that I too was musically gifted. Even before my teens I was given a lot of expensive training for my future great success writing musical comedies, both words and music; I would live at home and Mother would be my manager; marriage could wait until I was "established."

My mother was confident in her power over me until I reached puberty. Then sex became the greatest threat to her hopes. She acted as if there were no such thing, sending me to an all-girls high school and then, when I was only sixteen, to Barnard College, directly across the street from where we lived so that she could keep a close watch on her daughter. She did not know that I was already planning my escape. I wrote musical comedies for my mother and secret stories for myself about the tensions of my relationship with my family; when one was published in the Barnard literary magazine, I was afraid to bring a copy home. I came to think writing was like sex—an illicit and transgressive act.

Until I was eighteen and fell in love with an instructor at Barnard, I'd managed to live a double life fairly successfully. Donald Cook was ten years older, a former Columbia classmate of Allen Ginsberg's and Lucien Carr's, a connection to the world I would eventually enter when I met Jack. Donald was divorced, not Jewish, the father of a small child. He was the kind of brilliant man who could be intellectually stimulating and crushing all at once. He introduced me to bebop, marijuana, Mahler, Proust, and *Steppenwolf*; Allen Ginsberg, Carl Solomon (to whom Allen would later dedicate *Howl*), and William Burroughs turned up at his apartment. My affair with Donald was so all-consuming, it became impossible to conceal.

I was certain we would be married the moment I was out from under my parents' roof. I was wrong. After terrible scenes at home, I moved into a maid's room in an apartment a few blocks from Columbia on Independence Day, 1955. I was prepared to support myself entirely with my fifty-dollar-a-week secretarial job, even though it wasn't quite enough to live on. But my courage was not rewarded. Donald became more and more distant and soon took up with another Barnard student.

The life I had chosen for myself grew very dark. I went to bed one night with a Columbia boy I met at a party and became pregnant. As I went through the terrifying process of arranging to have an illegal abortion, I felt totally alone, not sure whether I would come out of this experience alive or why I was going to all this trouble to ensure my continued existence. When I later understood *Beat* in terms of its original definition— "exhausted, at the bottom of the world, but looking up or out"*—it seemed to me that in my own way I had reached that state of being even though I was a woman.

In *The Town and the City* I found a book about leaving home. I'd read it that fall with the feeling that the novel was reading me, that Kerouac could have told my story—the pain and guilt of breaking with my family, the driving need to do so. There was something in Kerouac's voice, the profound sadness and heartbreaking awareness of mortality underlying his driving energy, that made me know I could love him. He'd revealed so much of himself that he would not be a stranger if I ever got to meet him. But as much as Kerouac ever revealed, there would always be a whole subcontinent held back.

We were together for a year and ten months, though *together* is probably not the precise word to use. Jack could come and go in my life, turning up for a few weeks or perhaps a month, and each time he left I was never entirely sure I'd see him again. Off he'd go in search of the solution a new destination seemed to offer. But by 1957 there was no place on earth where Jack could be free of his own demons. He was a man who could only live moment by moment and who did not make promises, and in that way he was scrupulously honest and did no lasting harm. When he said, Good-bye until next time, he'd leave you with your freedom intact, whether you wanted that freedom or not.

*Allen Ginsberg's explanation, as quoted by John Clellon Holmes in "This Is the Beat Generation." Kerouac, also according to Holmes, called the Beat Generation "a generation of furtives."

Although our relationship proved to be less than I had hoped, for Jack, it became a far more significant part of his life than the passing encounter he and Allen Ginsberg had initially intended. Between Jack's visits to me in New York, we'd write to each other. In putting words down on paper, we became more than lovers—we became friends. ("I had me a companion there," he would later write in *Desolation Angels,* as if the experience were a novelty for him.) I did not want to admit to myself that love was very threatening to Jack; friendship was far more durable.

I'd found no indication in his semiautobiographical first novel of the convoluted nature of Jack's attachment to his mother, which both sustained and suffocated him. And Jack would never address the question of this bond directly. Instead he would express his philosophical fear of the maternal side of women—their power to bring new life (which he equated with the inevitability of death) into the world. By never staying with any woman very long, restlessly "digging" one after another as if they were interchangeable after the first sexual excitement, he'd remained faithful to Memere in his fashion. Each of Jack's affairs was like new territory to explore that would inevitably prove to have "bad vibrations."

No wonder the times we actually spent with each other always felt very fraught. My problem was that I deeply loved him; I wanted him, needed him, in all the embarrassingly conventional ways, a truth I worked hard to conceal. During each of his absences any glint of romantic feeling in his brotherly letters would reignite my hopes. Yet I always knew that Jack and I would never be "together" in the way other couples were. For the odd kind of relationship we were having, there were no models to go by, only what my own intuition told me—that I would have to learn to live like Jack did, moment by moment (or at least be able to fake it when my own needs felt overwhelming); that if I ever asked for more, he'd be gone. Whenever this began to get too painful, I'd remind myself that I was actually quite young. With so much time still stretching ahead of me, I could be with Jack like this.

He was a man whose feelings were constantly shifting. The Jack Kerouac who wrote to you last week would not be the same person who arrived on your doorstep. No one has had a deeper understanding than Virginia Woolf of what it means to exist in a state of flux. "What I write today, I should not write in a year's time," she observed in "A Sketch in Time." In the same essay she wrote, "I see myself as a fish in a stream; deflected, held in place; but cannot describe the stream." For Kerouac the stream had become a river in full flood. When he wrote, emotions coursed through him, changing from sentence to sentence, making his words as alive and vari-colored as the brush strokes in an Impressionist painting. But the price must have been very high. By the time I met him, Kerouac had become what W. B. Yeats once called in an essay about the modernist writers of his generation "a man helpless before the contents of his own mind." The flow had become too fast to sustain a life.

I remember Jack's silences, so deep you'd be afraid to break into them. And how he'd plunge into the blind, heightened intensity of drunkenness when he had to go out and meet the world. After the first thrill of success, his fame evoked fear and self-hatred. He'd take the phone off the hook and double-lock the door, and we'd hole up in my apartment like hunted outlaws. But I also saw him during the increasingly rare times he seemed in balance. Then his innate sweetness would be captivating. He'd lie on the floor on his belly, nose to nose with my cat Tigris as it ate from its bowl, or propose that he take me to Chinatown on a real "date," or lavishly praise a Lipton's soup I made for him, or sing along to Symphony Sid on the radio. He had the capacity to make the most ordinary things seem radiant. This was the real Jack, I'd tell myself—and I'd wish he could just stop right there and stay that way forever. I became intent on saving him through showing him that he was loved.

At twenty-one and twenty-two, I was much less experienced than I imagined. I'd grown up in a household without alcohol, except for the bottle of Manischewitz that appeared on the table at Passover. I worried terribly about Jack's drinking, but made the mistake of thinking he could control it if he could only find a home somewhere—a home that would include a woman, of course. The night I met him at Howard Johnson's, he told me he had recently spent sixty-three days in solitude as a fire watcher on Desolation Peak in Washington. He did not tell me he had tried to live without alcohol and had almost cracked up there. In fact, he still clung to the idea that he could solve everything if he wanted to by retreating to a shack in the woods and becoming a hermit. It was a long while before it became clear to me that he had reached a stage in his agony where he could neither be alone nor be with people, much less sustain a love affair.

"Why on earth (outside sickness and hangovers) aren't people CONTINUALLY DRUNK?" Jack asked the San Francisco poet Gary Snyder in a letter written three months before everyone in America knew his name. "I want ecstasy of mind all the time . . . if I cant have that, shit . . . and I only have it when I write or when I'm hi or when I'm drunk or when I'm coming."

Until I read the collection of published letters Jack wrote between 1940 and 1956, I believed that the publication of *On the Road*—with its lethal combination of fame, hero worship, notoriety, and abuse—had destroyed him. But the devastation had begun long before that. His letters showed me that after 1951, the year of his breakthrough into a new kind of spontaneous prose, there was a distinct change in him. The pursuit of that elusive, unfettered voice became everything. In the brief periods when Jack became its medium, he must have felt as self-sufficient as a god. Writing protected him from all his needs and doubts and failures. "I'm back in my starry element," Jack once wrote me when the words seemed to be flowing out of his typewriter.

I have come to believe that during the years when he was writing *The Town and the City* in a slow, steady, rather conventional way, Jack's work served as a stabilizing force in his life, the way it does for most greatly gifted writers. Following *On the Road*, however, Jack lost that fragile source of balance. Each new book would be blasted out of him, in short bursts of tremendous energy, as if he were a jazz musician ecstatically playing at the peak of his ability.* But such highs could only be short-lived. After each one, Kerouac would fall into a desolate valley, attempting to fill the void in himself with alcohol until he could find his way to the next peak.

As Maurice Blanchot has observed about the perils of automatic writing in *The Space of Literature*, "It is a matter of reaching the point where to speak is to say all and where the poet becomes the one who cannot withdraw from anything, who turns away from nothing, but is yielded up, without any protection whatever, to the foreignness and the measureless excess of being."

It did not help Jack that these were the years when no one would publish him, when he was not only poor but essentially homeless. *Bored* was the revealing word that began to crop up frequently in his letters. For Kerouac, boredom was always synonymous with despair. "Starving to death on the road many times," he wrote William Burroughs in 1954, "at least I was interested, looked forward to eating. But ennui, oh ennui, it's too much." He turned to Buddhism in a frantic effort to bring some balance back into his life; unfortunately, he misused it to justify his sense that his existence on earth had become loveless and meaningless.† Even writing had begun to seem empty. By the fall of 1956, when he decided to withdraw from the world to Desolation Peak, Kerouac had started to ask himself a writer's most dangerous question: Had he written himself out?

In 1960, after undergoing three years of a relentless barrage of ridicule and criticism that seemed aimed at silencing him, Jack found himself in an agonizing dry spell and contemplated giving up. On November 21, in a "Letter to Myself," he ascribed his reluctance to write "a true new novel" to his fear of letting people know what he was really thinking: "as soon as they find out they will all begin yelling at me again or pawing at me, for one reason or another." He seemed bitterly aware that he had lost much of the hard-

---

*During Kerouac's amazingly productive seven-year period preceding the publication of *On the Road*, he also wrote *Visions of Neal, Dr. Sax, Tristessa, Maggie Cassidy, Visions of Gerard,* and the first half of *Desolation Angels.*
†"Do you think you understand [Buddhism]?" Gary Snyder scolded Jack in a 1959 letter. "Nobody ever said anything against love or entanglement with women but you."

won confidence that had freed him to write unself-consciously. Now he was merely raw meat for legions of hack journalists: "Where for instance it was I myself who 'interviewed' others & asked them questions and gained thereby an interest in life and in the way of an author gathered life-material, now they are interviewing ME constantly because I'm a famous and 'rich' author and the bloody King of the Beatniks."

Our relationship has had a long and curious afterlife. Even if I had wanted to forget Jack Kerouac, our culture would not have allowed me to do so. Worshipped, reviled, misunderstood, and invoked perhaps more than any other twentieth-century American writer, he has become an archetype—more of an icon than a man who lived and breathed. I can hardly pick up a newspaper or magazine without suddenly coming upon his name. Is it true, I sometimes have to ask myself, that I actually once knew this Kerouac?

I have always had to prevent my memory of Jack from being swamped by legend. In recent years, I have also had to guard it from what others present as "fact"—Kerouac was gay, Kerouac was a racist, an anti-Semite—"biographies" written with dubious agendas out of a desire to capitalize on their shock value. I have read weird paraphrases of passages from *Minor Characters*, the memoir I published in 1983, in which each careless error and clumsy distortion seems calculated to show that what happened between us had no more substance than the bumping together of two strangers in a subway car.

In 1999, just as I was finishing this book, the second volume of Jack's selected letters (1957–1969) was published. I then had the disturbing experience of being able to read what Jack had written to his male friends during the course of our love affair—lines never meant for my eyes. The Jack who wrote Allen Ginsberg and Neal Cassady was boastful about his sexual escapades ("three girls in bed at once" was a dubiously frequent claim), and almost deliberately cold and uncaring in his references to me—especially when he was drinking and writing to Allen, who had little feeling for women. Of course, I was well aware that this was the way American males—not just the Beats—talked to each other in the 1950s, denying any emotional dependency upon the women in their lives. But I still found myself asking, was this the real Jack or a mask? Had the real Jack been cynically manipulative in his dealings with me? Or was he the one who later declared in *Desolation Angels*, "I still love her tonight"? How much fictionalizing was there in the letters Kerouac wrote to the people he knew, how much truth in his "real-life novels"? In a more objective mood, I had to accept that Jack's tenderness always coexisted with his despair and his fear of disappearing into the void he believed in. The Kerouac legend may be set in cement, but for me, the reality of the past keeps fluctuating, almost as if Jack were still alive.

Jack's prodigious ability to remember "everything" is now mythic. I remember being often bowled over by this faculty of his. Jack would begin telling a story about something that had happened, say, ten years ago and amaze me by his fluent recall of every nuance of a conversation. Each day I saw him mysteriously jot things down in one of the softcover black notebooks he had bought in Mexico City; he had a special notebook for his dreams. One of the most penetrating observations about Kerouac was made by his friend John Clellon Holmes: "Anyone who remembered everything would have to drink."

My own memory is much more pared down, shaped by my forgetfulness. And I have never kept a consistent written record of my life. Certain things in the past are clear to me as if they had just happened; other things seem unretrievable. I can tell you that Kerouac ate fried eggs for breakfast, but I cannot tell you exactly how we made love. He was gentle and warm and it was the feeling of connection with him that made me happy. I remember that on our first few nights together, Jack would leave me after we had made love and go into the back bedroom, open the window to let in the cold January air, and lie down on the floor in his sleeping bag. He believed this was beneficial to his health,* but it was a practice he soon abandoned.

"We were wonderful, healthy lovers," Jack wrote in *Desolation Angels*. I doubt that our lovemaking was "great," according to our current athletic standards of performance, but then little lovemaking was in the 1950s. Even for rebels, bohemians, and Beats, it was an act surrounded by anxiety—by the woman's fear of becoming pregnant or being thought bad or showing that she liked it too much or, worst of all, that she felt unsatisfied; by the man's fear of not proving himself or being "trapped." As such, it was laden with uneasy significance, far more momenteous—and less free—than it is today.

Some lost things have come fully back to me. In the fall of 1998, a package from the Kerouac estate arrived in the mail containing Xeroxes of all the letters I wrote to Jack over forty years ago. I'd always wondered if he'd kept them. In the two years I knew Jack, he was constantly on the move, never carrying more than a couple of changes of clothes and his notebooks in a cheap zipper bag. He never told me it was his practice to save all letters from his friends. Whenever he reached home base, wherever his mother Gabrielle Kerouac happened to be living—in Ozone Park, Long Island, or Rocky Mount, North Carolina, or Orlando, Florida—he'd file them carefully away with his journals to be used later as *aides-mémoire* when he wrote another volume of what he called "the Duluoz Saga," the fictional chronicle of his entire life. (His own letters were often warm-ups for passages in his books.)

I took the package upstairs and opened it and found myself face to face with the twenty-one-year-old I'd once been. I hadn't forgotten her, but there were ways in which she was subtly different from the young woman I remembered. The letters reminded me how tough she'd had to pretend to be in order to stay afloat, how orphaned she sometimes felt, and how badly she'd wanted the

---

*He was worried about a recurrence of phlebitis, and would also stand on his head every morning to "reverse the flow of blood" in his body.

commitment from Kerouac she had resolved never to ask for. I winced at the thought of all the rewriting I must have done, taking out the hurt parts, the phrases that might give me away, but suddenly I also remembered how, almost without my volition, my voice began to stretch and change, how my sentences began to seem less and less "composed"—the feeling of writing *up* to Jack in longer and longer breaths.

John Sampas of the Kerouac estate had warmly invited me to put our correspondence together in a book. As soon as I began interweaving Jack's letters and mine, I was struck by how our voices instantly began bouncing off each other, as if the dialogue we'd broken off in the fall of 1958 were still going on with all of its risky unspoken subtext. It would be a mistake for the reader to put too much emphasis upon what Jack Kerouac withheld from me and to forget what he'd had to give. He'd written to a very young woman as an equal, someone strong enough to take the truth. He'd generously recognized the writer in her. And he'd never boxed her in. This was rare for the sexist 1950s, even in Bohemian circles. Undoubtedly, Jack knew from the start that the open-ended relationship we had was really all he had to offer. But it didn't take me long to stop blaming him when it ended. He could behave unforgivably, yet you would ultimately have to forgive him. "Do what you want," Jack used to tell me. "Always do what you want."

I carried Jack's letters along with me for decades—through moves to various jobs and lofts and apartments, brief marriages to two other men, the birth of a child, an interrupted career as a novelist. Some were written in pencil on blue air-letter forms; some were typed in big black word blocks—sentences that refused to end and never looked back, written with the bald honesty I'd sometimes had to absorb like a blow. There was a battered white metal file that always moved with me. Jack's letters were somewhere in there, even if I could not immediately lay my hands on them. For many years no one else knew of their existence. I did not read them again until 1981, when I decided to write my memoir. I'd planned to quote from them, but in 1982, permission was denied by the late Stella Kerouac, Jack's widow, still grieving for Jack, who had died in 1969, and fiercely protective. The letters were part of my story, but unlike my memories, the words on the old pieces of paper did not belong to me.

I sold the originals a few years after my memoir was published. After all, they were only objects, like the Lee Wiley record we used to play or the paperback of *Fear and Trembling* Jack left behind in my apartment; the copies I kept were all I needed now. I spent the money to build something I never would have wanted when I was twenty-one, caught up in all the excitement of an oncoming cultural revolution. A small brown house on the edge of the woods. Jack would have approved, I thought, remembering his dream of finding a shack somewhere for himself. When I turn off the lights and stand on my porch at night breathing in the great hush of the dark, rustling trees, I often think how closely he would have listened to all the sounds of this vibrant silence.

Part I

.

March-April,
1957

THE NIGHT OF OUR BLIND DATE in January 1957, Jack couldn't even afford to buy me a cup of coffee—his last twenty had vanished earlier that day when he'd bought a pack of cigarettes and received change for a five—so I treated him to a hot dog and baked beans at Howard Johnson's. Then he came home with me to my first apartment. As we headed uptown in the subway, we both noticed a catchy new advertising slogan, FLY NOW, PAY LATER, which I found quite relevant to the beginning of this love affair. "You should call your novel that," Jack immediately suggested. (He seemed to like the idea that I too was a writer, although he disapproved of my admiration for Henry James.) We exchanged our first kiss as soon as we were inside my apartment. "I don't like blondes," Jack warned me, coming up for air, but I didn't take this as seriously as I should have.

I was living at the time in two furnished rooms on the ground floor of a brownstone on 113th Street between Broadway and Amsterdam. The following morning I successfully executed a breakfast of bacon and eggs on the rickety two-burner stove in a corner of the living room—cooking was one of my recently acquired skills. Jack had spent his first years in New York living all over this Columbia University neighborhood where I'd grown up, walking these streets discussing Proust and Nietzsche and the

"New Consciousness" with Lucien Carr, Allen Ginsberg, and William Burroughs while I was still in pigtails.

Now that I was drawn into Jack's world, it became harder and harder to show up at the MCA Literary Agency each morning. Nights had become long and sleepless, full of hard-drinking people of his acquaintance. We often went downtown to visit Lucien Carr, whom Jack considered his closest friend. They had met in 1944, when Lucien was a freshman at Columbia; it was Lucien, in fact, who had introduced him to Ginsberg and Burroughs. At nineteen, according to Jack, Lucien had looked like Rimbaud. But for years he had hidden his beauty behind horn-rimmed glasses with clear lenses and a wispy mustache. In 1944 there had been an incident that would cast a shadow over the rest of his life. On Riverside Drive, with his Boy Scout knife, Lucien had killed an older man named David Kammerer, who had been obsessed with him since his boyhood in Saint Louis and had followed him to Columbia. At Lucien's trial, prominent Columbia English professors had testified as character witnesses, and he had been sent to a reformatory for three years. In many ways, Lucien seemed more "settled" than Jack's other friends. He worked as a night editor for the United Press and had an elegant, weary-looking wife named Cessa and two small boys, who were fascinated by Jack. But I was often aware of an unsettling edge to Lucien's conversation, even though he could be very charming. He had made Jack promise never to write about him, or to mention the Kammerer case to members of the press.

After seeing Lucien, Jack would never be ready to go back uptown. We would make exhausting tours of the Village bars, running into subterranean characters like Stanley Gould or Bob Donlin, who seemed to be doing little with their lives except drinking and smoking marijuana.

It was always steadying to go to Elise's apartment in Yorkville and see Allen Ginsberg and Peter Orlovsky, who seemed almost like Jack's brothers. Allen, fresh from his triumphant readings of *Howl* in San Francisco, was like a brilliant, gleeful general, deploying his troops as he plotted a literary takeover: "Now Jack, tomorrow we're taking the bus to Paterson and going to see William Carlos Williams. . . ." Gentle, blond Peter would make tea for everyone and sweep the floor. They had a rather programmatic way of removing their clothes, but you got used to it, and it wasn't too different from being at the beach. Sometimes I worried about Elise because she'd been hopelessly in love with Allen for years, but she said she now loved Peter too. I knew I could never be as Beat as that.

Late one night as Jack and I were coming home from the Village, our subway car came to an abrupt jolting stop just as it began to pull into the Ninety-sixth Street Station. A man had jumped onto the tracks. As soon as the doors of our subway car opened, we fled the station and walked home. Jack was ashen, unable to speak, as if the suicide were an omen, or as if he'd been implicated in the death of this stranger.

During these first weeks of our relationship, Jack didn't seem especially excited about the forthcoming publication of *On the Road** in the fall and *The Subterraneans* the following spring. It seemed as if he'd waited too long. *On the Road*, especially, had become old to him; he'd moved on from there, written many other books since 1951, all of them "published in Heaven," as Allen had written in the dedication to *Howl*. Mostly he seemed to feel weary relief at the prospect of having a little money in his pocket. He told me how he'd promised his father that someday he'd buy his mother a house—maybe he'd really be able to do that eventually. He also hoped critics would admire his breakthrough into spontaneous, unfettered prose. Although there had been rumblings of unusual interest in the Beat Generation writers ever since Ginsberg's historic reading of *Howl* at the Six Gallery in San Francisco a few months before, Jack had no idea of the furor that would await him in September 1957.

For the time being, work on my novel came to a halt. Why was I writing about a silly college girl instead of something really important? The fact that I was getting a lot of encouragement from

*On January 11, Malcolm Cowley had finally—rather grudgingly—given Jack a contract to sign.

5

Hiram Haydn, the editor in chief at Random House (I'd begun the novel in a workshop he taught at the New School), only seemed to increase my uncertainty. What would it mean if Haydn actually bought it? Why should I have it so easy when Allen and Jack had found it so difficult to get published?

I'd begun to feel I was living at an incredibly accelerated speed. One of my bosses at MCA said he'd noticed a great change in me. He was sort of a dead soul who had wrecked the literary talent of his youth by becoming king of the True Confessions writers; sometimes he'd buy me drinks and morosely talk about the tragic mistakes he'd made for cash.

"Yes, something's happened to you, and I don't know what it is."

"I'm Jack Kerouac's girlfriend." I knew he'd been following the recent articles about the underground writers of the so-called San Francisco Renaissance.

He put his hand on my forehead. "Why, you're burning up," he said wistfully.

My weeks with Jack passed all too quickly, as far as I was concerned. Ahead, like a cement wall, his departure date loomed. Except for one night when he went to see his brunette ex-girlfriend Helen Weaver and stayed too long, and I made him come home with me—"It's her or me," I said, collecting him in a cab where he sat helplessly laughing at my audacity—we were getting along fine. But he had never planned to stick around. William Burroughs was waiting for him in Tangiers, ready to show him the manuscript of *Naked Lunch*, which Jack was going to type up for him, and Allen had already paid for his passage on a freighter.*

On February 15, Jack sailed for Africa.

■

---

*By the spring of 1958, Ginsberg, broke in Paris, would be rather perturbed by Jack's slowness in returning the $225.

[aboard the S.S. *Sloveniall*]
[early March 1957]

Dear Joyce—As I write this we're only 8 miles from the
African coast & will be in at dusk— It was a good thing you
didnt come back on the ship with me because it only went to big
gas tank barges off Perth Amboy— Also because I went to
Lucien's alone, they were able to squeeze me in at his mother's
little dinner, where I ate a pint of vanilla ice cream covered with
creme de menthe and been feeling good ever since— Our books
turned out fine—ten days at sea studying history & Kierkegaard
have opened new cracks in my mind—I'm saving *Genji* for
Spain— Fresh sea air, sleep, walking on deck, sun, & now I'm my
old self again (the healthy Jack you never saw)— Rarin to go in
Tangiers, the Blue Pearl of the Hesperides—the city of *vice!*
whee!

This is also by way of being a greeting to Allen, Peter, Ellyse
[*sic*] and [Sheila]*— All during the trip I ate alone at a huge
white tablecloth with one mysterious Yugoslavian woman Mata
Hari— We had a dangerous storm 500 miles out & almost
foundered. . . . in all my years as seaman I never saw my ship bury
its nose in mountain waves & plunge up into other valleys like a
rowboat. . . . it was awful, we had to flee South & lose a day—
During this ordeal, I heard the words:—
EVERYTHING IS GOD, NOTHING EVER HAPPENED
        EXCEPT GOD—and I believed & still do.
Kierkegaard & the storm together made me see this luminous
peaceful truth— You must read FEAR AND TREMBLING (never
mind SICKNESS UNTO DEATH, which is an abstract discussion
of despair)—F&T is about Abraham & Isaac & made me cry—
At moments I was sad remembering your tears—we'll meet
again—

Tangiers—wow! Immediately Bill Burroughs took me to the

---

*The pseudonymous Sheila, who had gone to Barnard with Elise and me, was living
with Elise in Yorkville.

Casbah where the veiled women pass— I was so high I thought I'd seen it all before— He lives on a hill overlooking the bay where even now I can see the S.S. Slovenia docked— We smoke marijuana right in the cafes, in public, it's legal—a strange wild Arab town—old as time—

Very excited I am— I'll get me a room of my own & write— bright sunshine this morning, cries of Arab peddlers, & tonight again the mysterious Casbah & that whanging music— Write soon & let me hear the latest. Love, Jack XXX

X
For
TiGris*

Monday, March 11, 1957

Dear Jack,

It was lovely to get your letter. You sound fine—absolutely golden. I'm glad.

I've had a frantic time of it this month—looking for a job. I finally have one, start Thursday. But guess where it is?—Farrar, Straus & Cudahy! I'll be working for [John] Farrar, who is a sweet, neurotic, tweedy old man, who dates back from the Maxwell Perkins days in publishing. I met him on Ash Wednesday, and he had an ash on his forehead. He said to me, "Don't be alarmed, Miss Glassman. It's only Anglican ash." I don't know whether this augurs good or ill, but anyway I'm delighted to be through with MCA. It's funny, but I think if I hadn't known you, I wouldn't have been ready to quit MCA yet. You and the great beautiful freedom you have reminded me of myself and what I really wanted—all of this had become terribly mixed up with snobbish, ridiculous, theatrical ideas of some vague kind of glittering power—but I don't want to be a literary agent, I'm too young, and besides I really do want to be a writer,

*A grey alley cat I'd hauled in from the street.

and I shouldn't get all involved with anything else. I know that getting another job in publishing doesn't sound to you like a very radical step, but the point is that this is just a nice, quiet job *that won't lead anywhere*—and I don't care! Now I can look at a job as something that pays the rent, keeps me alive—nothing more, and I can get up and walk out of it if I want to! For me this is somehow an enormous revelation.

I've thought a lot about your letter—about your finding God in the middle of the storm. I can't really comprehend that—I want you to know that about me. I scramble from day to day, hour to hour, and I seldom stop to ask questions, because when I do, I find everything in the world senseless, without reason, and it terrifies me. I am not defending myself; I am simply telling you this. I look at your way with wonder—but there is nothing I can say to you about it, except that. And in the meanwhile, I move two miles downtown to a new job, not too different from the old one, and you move across the ocean to another continent!

Shall I tell you some news? Allen and Peter sailed Saturday after being delayed for weeks because of the tugboat strike. Elise and [Sheila] are now taking over the negotiations about Nicky and Julius [Orlovsky]—all of which is awfully complicated and doesn't look too hopeful—Nicky is being uncooperative, saying that no one can prove him sane because he is sane, etc., which doesn't help much. I've met Lafcadio [Orlovsky], who's wonderful, interested and curious about everything: the first question he asked me was "Were you living with Jack?"; the first question he asked Elise was "When are you getting married?" —all this, while looking very stern and self-contained. The two Helen's are no longer talking to each other—Helen W.* moved out and Helen E.† asked me to live with her. I refused—I really do like being alone, except for having you around, which was fine. Elise won't move in with me, after all. The 1st issue of the Evergreen Review came today, and I guess the second will be along soon. I can't

*Helen Weaver, Jack's previous girlfriend.
†Helen Elliott, an old girlfriend of Lucien's, was sharing an apartment with Helen Weaver.

9

think of any other news. I will try to get to a Post Office this week and send you the two articles—I'm terribly bad about mailing things. It was funny to read about you: there you were all printed up, called a "frantic Buddha" and compared to Celine, *et al.*, and I remembered you leaning on a garbage can, eating pizza and saw your red shirt lying on the rocking chair, still smelling of you even though you were thousands of miles away.

Well, tell me all about the city of vice.

Love,
Joyce

■

It did seem a truly wild coincidence to land a job at Farrar, Straus & Cudahy. Two people there had important connections to Jack. The editor in chief was Robert Giroux, who had published Jack's first novel, *The Town and the City*, at Harcourt, Brace, wining him and dining him for a number of years but reacting with dismay when Jack came to his office and triumphantly unfurled the newly typed scroll of *On the Road*. In a blind rage, Jack had rushed out of Giroux's office, taking the scroll with him. When Jack later gave his editor a chance to read a retyped manuscript, Giroux had compared it to Dostoievsky, but said he was positive the company would reject it anyway on the grounds that it was too unusual and controversial. Jack was still quite bitter about this outcome.

Helen Weaver, whom Jack was still a little in love with, I suspected, worked in the production department of my new employer. Helen seemed to be my nemesis (or maybe I was hers), but I couldn't help liking her and we gradually became office friends, avoiding the subject of Jack.

Allen and Peter had set sail for Tangiers in early March. They delegated to Elise and her roommate Sheila, who had become Peter's girlfriend during their visit to New York, the responsibility of looking out for Peter's brothers. Nicky and Julius Orlovsky were both in mental institutions; Elise and Sheila were supposed to help Nicky get released—how, they didn't quite know. Elise was especially concerned about sixteen-year-old Lafcadio, who had been living with Allen and Peter in San Francisco and was now back in Northport, Long Island, with his mother in dangerously isolated circumstances.

■

[Tangiers]

MARCH [?] 19. . . . Dear Joyce: Only just got your letter* due to slow sloppy mailsystem at the American Legation . . . a month late. . . . From now on write to me at this hotel address . . . & I will get your letters in 4 or 5 days at most . . . very charming to hear from you, very pleased. . . . Allen is arriving here in a few days and we will row out in a boat to meet his ship . . . we row often, in the bay . . . I take long walks to see the ancient fishermen pulling nets with a slow dance . . . there are many dull expatriate characters here I try to avoid mostly . . . not too many good vibrations in Tangier and the Arabs very quiet send out no vibrations at all so I spend most of my time musing in my room . . . somehow can't write here but anyway that can wait . . . what I'm actually doing is thinking nostalgic thoughts of Frisco . . . not too interested in this oldworld scene, as tho I'd seen it before plenty . . . anyway in early April I'm off by myself to Paris, the others can join me later, to get cheap garret . . . then London, Dublin, Brittany . . . then I try to get job on freighter, work my way back this summer . . . I just dont seem interested, got too much to do in America, shouldna come at all of course . . . so I'll likely be seeing you in NY in July maybe . . . look forward to seeing you, lonely here, dont like whores anyway and no girls speak English . . . mostly fags abound in this sinister international hive of queens . . . have had everything in the books, smoked opium, ate hasheesh, don't want any of it, just musing in my room, lights out, face sea, moon, liquid lights of anchored ships in bay, good

*The letter Jack refers to was lost.

enuf . . . the blink of lonely headland lighthouse. . . . Grove Press really pulled a fast one on me and cut the novel subterraneans by 60 per cent of all things and ruined swing of prose so I wrote and called it off . . . I will not stand for any more of this castration of my careful large work by liverish pale fag editors . . . you know my first novel Town and City in original ms. form was 1100 pages and ranked with five of the greatest books ever writ in America (this I believe) but after Harcourt Brace cut it over 50 percent to save paper, and ruined rhythm of sentences, it was like 2 or 3 thousand any-other novels a lil better than average . . . so the time has come to put my foot down on this editorial activity . . . no such action goes on in France, where young writers are pub- lished in toto . . . only the french have nothing to say because the Old World is weary. . . . You said you would airmail Nation and Village Voice articles, or did you, or is Allen bringing them any- way? . . . O well who cares, they say this and that about a writer but it doesn't prevent them from trying to castrate too. . . . Oh, I reckon by now you got my first letter to you? about the trip on the boat and the big storm and Yugoslavian woman I ate with and the books I read? curious to know, when you answer, let me know if you got that okay. . . . Your story about Five Spot amusing and the story about Tigris eating dandelions, what a cat (daf- fodils). . . . I'm curious to visit Brittany and find out what my father changed the name Keroach for, because I see there was a Breton Admiral called Ronarc'h so that it would be Keroac'h if he was correct. . . . On sunny mornings I sit crosslegged on my patio and read diamond sutra facing the Catholic priests of nearby church who stand in gangs reciting their rosaries facing the sea but I face the Heliolithic sun, hor. . . . Sometimes I spend all night comparing my newfound utter listless dispiritedness and no- care of where I am, what I do, to enthusiasm of old American writers like John Muir, Timrod, Twain, etc., the vigorous activi- ties of other men abashing me, as tho I had never written a line myself. . . . But since found out, we were all poisoned by the hasheesh, which has arsenic in it, because of spray, so that explains my so-far dispirited visit in Tangier and feeling of no vibrations. . . . I drink most delicious wine in the world, which costs 28 cents a quart, Malaga, sweet molassey wine from Malaga across these straits in Espagna. . . . Vision one afternoon: "All things that move are God and all things that dont move are God," and at the reutterance of this ancient secret all things that moved and made noise seemed to suddenly rejoice and all things that didnt move seem pleased! . . . Eat in marvelous French restaurant serving everything great, for one dollar, four courses, amazing menu, truffle casserole in cheese, etc., dainty pastries, impossible hors d'oeuvres, a pretty white cat sits on my lap as I eat, the proprietor insists I finish all my potatoes. . . .

Write soon, honey Love
Jack

■

I remember being taken aback by Jack's matter-of-fact line, "dont like whores anyway and no girls speak English." It was as if he'd forgotten for a moment whom he was writing to; our friendship was certainly quite different from the ones he had with Lucien or Allen. But I decided not to probe into the question of whether or not Jack was seeing other women—a policy I would later try to stick to with much greater difficulty. I had to keep reminding myself that I couldn't really wait for Jack to come back to me, since who knew if he would?

All at once I'd begun to meet many new people—the painters and poets who congregated at a nondescript-looking bar on University Place called the Cedar Tavern not far from the Union Square offices of Farrar, Straus & Cudahy. For years the Cedar had been the haunt of Jackson Pollock, who had died in a car accident in 1956, and other abstract expressionist painters. I began walking down there each day on my lunch hour and was soon introduced to Franz Kline and Willem de Kooning and a younger group of artists and writers, including Fielding (Fee) Dawson, Basil King, John Chamberlain, and Joel Oppenheimer, who had all studied at Black Mountain.

Black Mountain was a small arts college in North Carolina, where the educational experience had evidently been so heightened, incestuous, and intense that nobody who'd gone there could ever stop talking about it. When the institution went spectacularly bankrupt in 1956, a small group of diehards had stayed on, keeping warm by burning chairs in fireplaces, eating steaks stolen from the local supermarket. Finally the diehards had given up—half of them driving west toward the San Francisco Renaissance in North Beach, half of them heading north for downtown Manhattan and the Cedar. The final issue of the *Black Mountain Review*, due to be published early in 1958, would feature a contribution from Jack: "The Essentials of Spontaneous Prose." There was something about Jack's theories about bop prosody that reminded me of the new action paintings I was seeing, where the colors seemed danced upon the canvas in vibrant strokes with surprising explosions and little showers of paint as delicate as rain.

Many of my new acquaintances didn't live in apartments like most New Yorkers. Instead they inhabited old commercial lofts illegally, hiding their mattresses in ingenious ways in case a building inspector came to check the premises. On Friday nights, everyone turned up at openings at the cooperative storefront galleries on Tenth Street, where works by unknown artists excluded from the snooty galleries uptown were being exhibited in exuberant group shows. The next stop would often be the Five Spot, the new Bowery jazz joint whose walls were covered with flyers from the neighborhood galleries. I began going there with Elise. We'd buy our 25-cent beers and listen to John Coltrane. We were there the unforgettable night Billie Holliday suddenly stood up at her table and sang as Mal Waldron played the piano. (She had recently been deprived of her cabaret card by the police.) I'd always longed to go to Paris—the destination of the heroine in the novel I was writing—but now there was something in the air that made New York seem the most exciting place in the world.

■

Dear Joycey—

Am now leaving for Paris & Allen & Peter will take over my lovely patio room—"April in Paris" is all I keep singing (AT LAST)— Your vision of the Casbah, with palm trees and Legionnaires riding through, must come from an old Ronald Colman movie!—it's really called the *Medina* (The Casbah is the walled fort, cobblestones with one antique cannon), the Medina is full of narrow damp alleys, robed Arabs, vegetable stands, smoke of frying fish & Allen Ginsberg wandering around looking for asparagus—(romantic enough)—When I said "God" in my vision in the sea I didn't mean a bearded man in Heaven, I meant THAT WHICH PASSES THROUGH ALL ("Should anyone looking at an image or likeness of that which passes through all claim to know that which passes through all and should offer worship and prayer thereto, you should consider such a person an idolater who does not know truly that which passes through all." DIAMOND VOW OF WISDOM)—Then "Do not think the opposite either that when that which passes through all passes through knowing perfectly through all, it is not by means of its ability to pass through various kinds of excellent form. . . . [you] should neither grasp after such verdicts of the appearance of things nor reject them."

—Which, if you said it to the college crowd, would pass through one ear and out the other, as is proper and fitting— What are you doing at Farrar, Straus? Met Giroux yet? You might tell Giroux for me that Andre Deutsch, a new English house, has just bought *On the Road* & tell Bob that I'll go to London & look up Frank Morley—(Christopher's brother)— Is Helen Weaver still at F. Straus?— What a blue sea out there today, the cerulean blue I always dreamed for the Mediterranean— Today I'm making a reservation on the packet to Marseilles, then hitchhike to Paris— Who is going to be your publisher for your novel?— Yesterday I hiked 10 miles alone & climbed mountain, & sat on hillsides watching Berber villages— At night, flutes over the rooftops— Be seeing you in New York before 4th of July

Love, Jack

April 14, 1957

Dear Jack,

How is April in Paris—I guess you're there by now—I saw it in the newsreel last night: fireworks, dancing on the Seine, processions and crowds. Is it really like that? You were right—I guess my vision of the Casbah was more a vision of Hollywood than anything else.

April is cold here, with snow dropping shamelessly on the forsythias in Central Park, which isn't fair. But Columbia is very green and sleepy already.

What I am at Farrar, Straus is an "editorial secretary." I type, read manuscripts, etc. Quite peaceful. My boss is Mr. Farrar, an old man left over from the 20's (I read some poetry written in his heyday in '24—"I'll filch the golden pollen / From half a million bees, / And I'll dust it on some quiet bloom / Before she even sees." Etc., etc.—awful!) But he's a sweet old guy, suspects me of being "somewhat of a rebel"—he invited me to go to the P.E.N. Club tomorrow and asked me would I mind not wearing slacks— which is what he thinks all female rebels wear—so, dressed as *comme il faut* as possible, I shall go there and dig what happens to you when you become an old established writer. Mr. Giroux with his large, heavy white head is very very impressive. So far we have just mumbled good morning at each other and once he corrected my punctuation. Jack, he makes me feel terribly shy for some reason. Helen Weaver is still at FSC—we've become office friends, which is nice. The funny thing is that she's going out with Donald Cook now (remember, you met him in the West End and said he had an urchin's face) and I had gone around with him for two years. Incest again! The good thing about FSC is that for two hours each afternoon, I have nothing to do, and so I've appropriated that time to work on the book. I'm writing faster now, revising less, and there is much more dialogue, and I'm finally getting used to the sound of my own voice and finding out that I have one. Hiram Haydn is still interested and my agent is going to tackle him for an option when the workshop is over. If I don't get one, she wants me to try for a Houghton Mifflin Literary Fellowship.

How lovely about the English edition! Has anything more happened with Grove Press* —or is that deal completely finished? Are you writing A DHARMA BUM IN EUROPE now?

I went to hear Miles Davis, who is playing at the Cafe Bohemia in the Village. He's really fine—beautiful crazy lines floating on top of each other. He stood up very straight and looked stern. The place was packed, but silent as a cathedral— everybody at the bar looked sad and a little apprehensive and there was a weeping girl with a cat's face wandering back and forth looking for jazz musicians. Then—all of a sudden, a car smacked up across the street between a house and a lamppost. The people in the front seat were trapped but giggling. A man at the bar cried "Crazy!" threw up his arms and ran out into the street, followed by everybody except Miles Davis who kept playing. He finished and said quietly, "Thank you for the applause," and walked off. It was like a dream. I felt a little sick and went all the way uptown to Columbia and found the cat sleeping with his eyes open and rolled back into his head. I read some Jane Austen and went to bed and had a dream about being put into a prison for wayward girls and not being able to get out ever because it was supposed to be good for me.

Aside from the dream, I find that I've been pretty calm and happy for around four consecutive months now, which is sort of a record for me. Don't know why and won't ask too many questions. I'm not a questioner and not a believer either—that's all I meant when I wrote you about your vision of God (not a bearded man in heaven!). You are both a believer and a seeker, and to me it is the ability to seek or believe that is important, not what is

*The publishers of *The Subterraneans*.

17

sought or believed in. Is this any clearer? I've read and reread what you quoted from the Diamond Vow of Wisdom many times and the meaning keeps expanding and expanding.

Hope Paris is as beautiful as the songs promise and as wild as Henry Miller and that you are happy.

Are you really coming back in July? It would be great to see you.

Love,
Joyce

P.S. Am sending you the article Louise Bogan wrote on Frisco writers.

Would have written sooner, but wanted to wait till you got to Paris. Superstitious about the mails & American legations, etc. Very silly!

4/15 Since writing this I've gone [to PEN] & discovered it's much better to remain a *young* unestablished writer, if you're going to end up that stuffy!

Part II

.

May-August,
1957

A T THE END OF APRIL, I came home from work one evening and found a notice from Western Union in my mailbox. When I called their office, they read me a cable from Jack. He was returning to the States, already at sea on the SS *Nieuw Amsterdam:* Could he stay with me?

DOOR WIDE OPEN, I answered in the cable that reached him in the middle of the Atlantic.

I was thrilled, of course, to have Jack back so soon. I'd expected to lose him to Paris, to some dark-eyed Parisienne who looked a lot like Helen Weaver or some spoiled Vassar girl on her year abroad, lurking at a table in Les Deux Magots. My imagination was all too vivid. To fortify myself against disappointment, I'd started seeing other men, as if I really had managed to stop waiting.

But I remember feeling puzzled as well. It had been so important to Jack to go to France, the land of his Breton ancestors. He'd been planning to look up the ancestral Kerouacs in La Bibliothèque Nationale and to stay in Paris until July. Why had he left so quickly, the way he'd suddenly fled Tangiers?

Jack didn't have much to say about Paris the day he rang my doorbell and walked back into my life with his zipper bag. He'd seen Gregory Corso there, had a lot of trouble finding a place to stay, ended up in a miserable room in a Turkish whorehouse, got fed up with the unfriendly French, and went to London to visit his old prep school friend Seymour Wyse. He said he'd been homesick for America; he wanted to sit by a kitchen window and eat a bowl of Wheaties.

I'd cleaned the whole apartment, bought daffodils, washed my hair. I told him how great New York had become; I wanted to take him right away to all the downtown places I'd discovered while he was gone—the Cedar, the Five Spot. . . . I can't remember whether or not we went. What I do remember is the painful news Jack gave me: this time he wasn't going to stay with me more than a week. The woman I was losing him to was Gabrielle Kerouac; it was his mother's kitchen window that he'd longed for. He was going to pick up Memere in Orlando, Florida, a town that bored him profoundly—just swamps and mosquitoes, he said—and move her all the way to Berkeley, where he planned to rent a small house and settle down with her.

He wanted to live with his *mother?* Having struggled so hard to get away from mine, I couldn't believe it. I went into the bathroom to cry, which didn't fool him a bit.

But later Jack said, "Why don't you come out to San Francisco, if you want to. You can get your own place there, and then we can see each other all the time."

By the time he left, I'd made up my mind to meet him in California that summer. It was time for me to start my own travels anyway; the farthest I'd ever been from New York City was Cape Cod.

■

[Postcard from Berkeley, California]
May 15, 1957

Dear Joyce

This is my new permanent home, fine furnished apartment for only $50 a month, including utilities—so like I told you, rents are cheap in Frisco and you and Elise will have no trouble finding a place in the city— Berkeley is 8 miles away, the Univ. of Calif. campus—a little too quiet for an adventuresome twosome— Frisco (that is, North Beach) is jumping, millions of poets & jazz clubs & novelists 19 years old— FLY NOW, PAY LATER is a *sensational* title— Great! Use it! Hope you can recover Tigris, wish I was there to climb around back fences— Waiting for my type-writer to write you regular letters— Trip over with my Ma was a great adventure, and we were very fortunate.

Love, Jack

[Berkeley, California]
[late May, 1957]

Dear Joyce

Got your fine letter*—Yes, we'll find you some place to stay in the city when you get here, I'll meet you at the bus station (or at some pre arranged bar) and I'll carry your bag and we'll go find a room maybe where Allen used to live, called Monkey Block, or other places in North Beach, the SF Greenwich Village— I'm still waiting for the movers to arrive with my clothes before I get a little part time job, meanwhile been painting and writing haikus and taking short hikes with Phil Whalen—†

I saw Neal [Cassady] here, who is become mindless, borrowed $10 from me, made no explanation for not coming to get me, disappeared, and now his wife‡ writes a vituperative letter saying I'm a bad influence on her poor innocent hubby . . . so you see it's sinister everywhere. . . .

However, here the climate is great and getting better.

It'll be a good place to finish your book.

As for Elise, if she wants to go to Univ. of Calif., Berkeley is chockful of rooms and apartments, my mother and I found an ideal one in one hour of strolling in the leafy streets. I have a

---

*Evidently lost.

†Jack's close friend—one of the few Memere wholeheartedly approved of—was a San Francisco poet.

‡Evidently, Carolyn Cassady was not happy to hear that Jack planned to introduce Neal to Elise and me when we arrived in San Francisco. I had no idea that she and Jack had had a love affair with Neal's consent. (Neal Cassady had inspired the character Dean Moriarty in *On the Road*. A letter Cassady wrote Jack in 1950 was the catalyst for Jack's breakthrough into spontaneous prose.)

wonderful bedroom with high ceiling and furniture and big double bed, only waiting for my typewriter, books and manuscripts
now to complete the scene. At night I pace in my own little yard
in the dark. . . .

I got a letter from my ex-wife who says she wants to settle out
of court, wants me to sign a divorce paper merely, so she can get
remarried and her new husband will adopt child, and says in writing she doesnt want a cent.

So that will be that and maybe you were right when you said
the world *would* leave me alone to meditate and work in peace in a
hut in the woods. Five years of that and I'll be ready to teach the
world something it's dying to know. A little self-discipline. I'd like
to go to Montmartre again, in about five years, live there a year.

Has there been any new news about On the Road in NY?
Sterling Lord* seems to be scared of me now and doesnt write
any more.

I'm afraid Rust Hills† was not sincere, I had one of my friends
send him mountainclimbing and jazz poems and he wrote back
saying he wasn't interested in moutainclimbing and jazz, knowing
full well I am. That's my last "lunch" with such eager beavers;
why on earth do they want to OGLE at writers?

You'll love it here, it's great . . . there are art museums,
beaches, glorious parks, those Chinese restaurants, wharves,
waterfront, all kinds of interesting scenes and people, lotsa jazz,
friends to make. Just ignore me, my gloom, unless I feel better
when you get here.‡

Well, I guess Tigris is on his way to China, where he will
become an immortal and ride away on a dragon . . . always
knew it.

---

*Sterling Lord was Jack's literary agent.
†Hills was the fiction editor at *Esquire*.
‡"I have a blonde novelist following me from NY also a brunette (Ginsy's old girl) who
will liven up the North Beach scene maybe . . . anyway, orgies . . . After all this world
travel I feel infinitely dreary and dont know what to get excited about any more and
cant live without exuberance," Jack wrote Gary Snyder on May 25.

Has Elise heard from Allen? I sent him important papers to mail for me, I only wanta know if he's still in Tangiers now.

Today is Sunday in Allen's lil old rosecovered cottage, red flowers, red roses, weeds, mint, trees, fences, cats, ash cans, hanging rugs, ferns, bushes, backs of houses and blue sky.

What a fascinating letter. Till I hear from you, sweetie.

As ever
Jack

p.s. You dont know what to say to me
    because the kingdom is within . . .
    flesh and blood's a dream . . .
    so you fly now, pay later, all of us . . . I mean actually it's
PAY NOW, FLY LATER

■

While staying with me in New York, Jack had learned that his ex-wife Joan Haverty was looking for him. I heard of her existence for the first time during his short visit. Jack told me he'd never seen the little girl who had been born nine months after the breakup of their brief marriage (the father was some Puerto Rican guy, he claimed) and that he'd been jailed once for his refusal to pay alimony. He showed me a snapshot of a beautiful dark-haired child on a tricycle; "She's not my daughter," he said. But anyone could see that little Jan's resemblance to him was unmistakable, and I told him so.

He was a man who loved other people's children, but refused the role of father. He strongly suspected that I too, like any other woman, would want to bring new life into the world. Why give birth to a child who was only going to suffer and die? Jack's most painful early memory, in fact, was the death of his older brother Gerard—the event that had bound him for life to his griefstricken mother. Jack could accept his overwhelming responsibility for Memere, but for no one else. What he feared most was a loss of the freedom that enabled him to write. Freedom—during Jack's years of poverty and insecurity—was the only capital he had.

I too had "rejected" a child—the one I'd had scraped out of me. So there were ways in which I could understand why Jack could not bring himself to acknowledge the little girl in the photograph. But surely he'd want to know her someday, I thought, if life became easier for him.

Joan Haverty, who badly needed the child-support money Jack had no hope of earning with his writing, had made him feel like a hunted man, who could be arrested at any time and sentenced to the living death of a menial full-time job. But there had also grown to be something paranoid in Jack's fear of his ex-wife, in the way he wrote about her in his letters to his friends, associating her with the police. In the spring of 1957, he took elaborate steps to make Joan think he was still abroad, airmailing the letters he wrote her to Allen so that they could be sent back to the States with a Casablanca postmark. These were the "important papers" he alludes to in his letter to me.

Considering Jack's otherwise enthusiastic response to being back in California, I was unable to account for his gloomy mood. But the dark feelings any communication with Joan Haverty stirred up undoubtedly made even Berkeley seem "sinister." Still, the tone of Jack's first letters from the Coast suggested that he was managing to stay sober a good deal of the time as he worked on a revision of what would eventually become the first section of *Desolation Angels*, about his recent experiences as a fire watcher and his descent from his mountain solitude into the frenetic scene of the San Francisco Renaissance.

After receiving Jack's letter, I began to prepare for my momentous journey to the West Coast. In order to economize, I gave up my apartment and moved in with Connie Robins, a friend who worked at Farrar, Straus & Cudahy and lived upstairs, trying to save some money to tide me over in San Francisco until I found a new job there. I was also hoping to hear from Hiram Haydn before I left New York because I had finally sent him the first fifty pages of my novel, agonizing over every sentence in a way Jack would have thoroughly disapproved of.

It was embarrassing to be moving so slowly when Jack seemed so eager to have me with him, but although I longed to be in San Francisco, I was too innately cautious to go on the road impetuously and find myself in a situation where I lacked the resources to be self-sufficient. Would Jack really be there waiting, I could not help wondering, when I got off the Greyhound bus on the other side of the continent?

■

[Berkeley, California]
June 11, 1957

Dear Joyce

Your last letter* was charming— Anxiously awaiting your coming out here now, but not only me, Neal too, who wants to meet Elise and also [Sheila] if she's coming, wants me to relay the message that he's PLEADING for the girls to hurry up, he's so lonely etc. and says he's all ready for a great new season.†

Allen is in the papers almost every day now, including enclosed tidbit which you can give to Elise to mail Allen in her next letter— There are editorials in the papers and everything, bemoaning the Big Brother attitude of the local dumb Irish cops who, because the government in Washington closed the case,‡ took things into their own hands and are making fools of themselves.

I got big letters from Allen and Peter the other day describing what they've been doing—I'll save them all for Elise and [Sheila]. Tell Lafcadio Jack said for him to sit down and write his lonely brother Peter and tell him what's up.

---

*Another lost letter.

†Although I never said so to Jack, I was a little leery of meeting Neal, who according to Jack was much wilder than he was, and a frantic womanizer.

‡A reference to the Supreme Court decision on the *Howl* obscenity trial. The San Francisco authorities had raided the City Lights bookstore, confiscated the copies of *Howl,* and charged Lawrence Ferlinghetti and his store manager with selling an obscene work.

As you can see my typewriter's arrived, all our stuff, and my room looks real nice. Incidentally Don Allen* is also coming out here in July and wants us to find him a pad . . . there are plenty of them in Berkeley, as to the City I have a slew of experts in our bar, The Place, which is the main hangout, has clippings about Howl on the bulletin board and paintings and phonecalls and letters from friends that the bartender holds for you—You will love this mad joint, nothing like it in New York—I even got into a fight in there the other night because a little man with glasses was hitting his wife, he tried to hit me and I just held him by the arms and dumped him sitting on the floor—There are mad parks where we all sit with wine and look at the water—It's quite a gay mad scene, but I spend most of my time in quiet flowery Berkeley trying to write—I painted a lot but my enthusiasm is limited because I realize I'm really a word painter—I did some beauties though and maybe someday I'll go mad and paint stacks (would like to afford oils and real canvases)—Glad to hear Helen Eliot [*sic*] not mad at me, send her my love, also Helen Weaver, why not?—We all die and there's nothing to be bugged about—Yes, it looks like my wife only wants a divorce, an "absolute" divorce in Juarez, Mexico, I sent her the signature— Well, dont be sad in June New York, enjoy . . . the next time you live in NY live in the Village, Columbia Campus has become unutterably dreary, look at the West End† for instance . . . Is Stringham‡ coming out? "Ghostly lovers on television" is a beautiful phrase of yours, use it in FLY NOW PAY LATER. . . . As to Sinatra, he's made some great new records, I Wont Dance, The Lonesome Road, etc.— Glad to hear Connie is sweet to you— How do you like my latest haiku

---

*The editor in chief of Grove Press, which planned to publish *The Subterraneans* in 1958, and of the new *Evergreen Review*, whose second issue was going to be devoted to the San Francisco scene.
†The bar where Jack had hung out with Ginsberg, Carr, and Burroughs when he lived in the Columbia neighborhood in the 1940s.
‡Ed Stringham, who worked for the *New Yorker*, was a mutual friend of ours. I'd met him during my relationship with Donald Cook.

The Golden Gate

creaks

With sunset rust

It's the end of the land, babe, it gives you that lonely feeling—I KNOW that I'll eventually return to NY to live

Mad Jack

Important P.S.: Yes bring winter clothes to Frisco, it's very chilly
and dry all summer, never hot, a bit on the cool side always

June 11, 1957

Dear Jack,

Thought you'd like to have the enclosed about ON THE
ROAD from the Sunday Times; it's a good omen, I think—Breit's
column is sort of a weather vane. Anyway, I hope it will help you
feel a little easier about things.

Elise got another (later) letter from Allen and Peter, but still
isn't sure whether they're in Madrid or not—this one came from
Tangiers also. She read it to me, and they sound sad and discon-
nected just like you did. I have a hunch they'll be back this Fall.
Elise may not come out to SF—she doesn't know exactly what
she wants to do, maybe just a long leisurely trip across the country and then back to New York. But then there are days when she
wants to go to San Francisco after all. She's living down on the
lower East Side and I've been roaming around there a lot with
her, seeing strange streets—one was a street where tombstones
were made, a whole city of them behind a high wire fence,
clotheslines flapping over them, and boys playing ball on the
sidewalk. Also, I go down to the Five Spot with her occasionally.
They're having a boom because of an article in Esquire this
month, the one with pictures of Allen and Gregory [Corso]—but
the jazz hasn't been good, all percussion and nothing cutting
through it. Many college kids go there now, all of whom seem to
be fantastically blond and tall—they get up and dance with a
look-we-are-dancing look on their faces. One of the girls got up
while the music was playing, walked over to the platform, look-

ing as if she were going to interrupt the musicians to ask a question, but instead peered intently at something tacked on the wall, walked back to her young man and said with great satisfaction: "It's upside down."

I'm settling down in an unsettled sort of way with one foot on the bus already. The novel's been upset somehow for a while, and I wish I could get back with it.—No word yet from Haydn, but that's not the reason. I'm writing a short story to keep busy.

One day, Elise and I decided to try the fly-now-pay-later plan. We made a pact that if it could be arranged with the airline, we'd take off immediately. But it turns out that you need credit, and they investigate you for ten days to see if you're reliable, which is all very dreary and disappointing. So I'm still here with fifty dollars in the bank, and I'll tell FSC that I'll be leaving July 15th. I wish I had a million dollars for about two weeks. I'd spend it recklessly despite all that my parents ever taught me. They're being appropriately cautious,* but they're not flipping, thank God. They're full of helpful little suggestions like I'd better have five hundred dollars along with me, etc.

Love,
Joyce

[Berkeley, California]
[mid-June, 1957]

Dear Joyce,

Pacing up and down my yard yesterday I bethought myself about you . . . dont know how to say this so I'll just say it honestly— (1) I don't want you to be disappointed by San Francisco but it's really nowhere, in the few weeks I've been here I've been stopped 4 times and my name taken down 4 times for walking in the street after midnight (one time fined $2 for "going thru a red light") and as you know there's all this other cop trouble

---

*I had told them only that Elise and I were planning to go to the Coast together, not mentioning Jack.

impounding people's poetry books* and God knows what'll happen to Evergreen Review No. 2 which also has HOWL in it or Gregory's book of poems GASOLINE or anything in this mad silly stupid place which is now a culture for old people on retirement, cops prowling around all night to keep the streets absolutely quiet, in other words to prevent anyone from having fun—In short I am slowly being driven out of California which I loved when I first got here because it was so wild, so end-of-the-landish and has now fallen into the hands of Total Police Authority (God help us if this really spreads back East—in fact I foresee now (unless New York remains too big and wild and ungovernable and I can live there fairly as I please, as of yore) I can foresee being driven out of America altogether and will have to settle in Mexico.) My mother and I have already decided to return to New York, by Xmas, probably as early as October, and also of course the lift of police trouble from my wife enables me now to go back there fairly safe unless she has something else up her sleeve, tho I dont care because all I have to do is order a blood test†— But anyway, I'm thinking of YOU, coming out here and then seeing me leave in a few months . . . and also I'm broke and dont have much money to go into Frisco much, unless I get a little job soon, which I dont really want unless a newspaper sports job (which may be offered me soon)— I dont want you to come out here and be disappointed altogether, wasting your time and money— Who knows, maybe it would be better if you went with Elise on that $75 deal to Europe, at least you'd see something new—there's nothing new, out here, just the same old crap you hate so much about Columbia Campus—except for the nice weather which isnt important at all, it's the PEOPLE that count— Joyce, dont think for a minute that I don't want to see

---

*A second edition of Allen Ginsberg's *Howl*, which had been printed in England for City Lights Press, had been impounded by customs on the grounds of obscenity while Jack was in Tangiers.

†He was truly convinced at the time that a blood test would prove he was not Jan Kerouac's father. When he finally was ordered to have one in 1961, the results were inconclusive. Nonetheless, he was ordered to pay Joan Haverty $52 a month for child support.

you, I do, but I cant help it if when you come out here you'll be in tears of disappointment or just gloom, it's just awful— Of course we do have our goodtimes like I told you about, wine on the beach, but every time you turn around someone's gone to jail or in trouble with the cops BECAUSE of innocent things like that, the police have just absolutely got out of hand here, old people sit at home in front of their television sets and the streets are supposed to be DESERTED and are rapidly becoming deserted— What action there is in the streets of North Beach is under the most intense police surveillance (and even FBI) I've ever seen in all my born days— As an objective friend I would definitely not advise you to come out here, but to either stay in NY, move to the Village, or go to France with Elise, or go to Mexico even, where at least you can have fun—as a subjective amant, of course, I'd want to see you and love you all over again— Here's what I'm going to do: when ROAD comes out and I get another advance (I hope) I'm moving my mother back to New York, where anyway she can work 2 days a week and support herself completely, and then I'm going to Mexico to make me a pad, Mexico City, and will spend my time, the time of my life, alternating between Mexico City and New York City with occasional visits to this West Coast to see people and camp a little, and if I have the money trips overseas, but I shall never live in California, I can see it now, you dont realize how awful they've made it—there'll be bloodshed around here for sure— Imagine one woman writing in the paper if Jesus Christ was alive he would have led the police to the bookstore to impound HOWL! and all that kind of negative oldwoman atti- tude all over the place with all these new dreary neat cottages and clean streets with white lines and signs that say WALK, STOP, DONT WALK . . . I cant stand it. . . . I admit I'm flipping and am bugged everywhere I go but I cant make it here. I wish I hadn't painted such glowing pictures of this shithouse to you, and made you decide to throw everything up for a lark where you cant lark— But Joyce, if you do insist on coming out here, and get a job, then when I'm ready to leave we can go to Mexico together, that's why I say we could do that from New York after Xmas, it would be nice to be with you in Mexico City,—if you insist on coming out anyway please dont blame me any more, or by then dont blame me, now you're forewarned, and maybe you'll have a better time than I do anyhow. As for that glorious wild Neal, the cops long ago took his license because he drives like a human being, or like a young man, instead of like an old man half blind, so he's completely halted in his activities and we cant afford to see each other. That and many other similar stories. If you can go to Europe with Elise, good God do it, you'll really be doing something! Besides I can join you and Allen and everybody there in Paris, probably within a year— Let me know what you think, study the matter, I'm just warning against a possible mistake that I myself started, damn it. As for seeing YOU, that's alright with me anytime, because I really like you, you're a real kid, that is, a true heart. . . . Thanx for the big interesting letter, write

Jack

(But you decide and you

always do what you want

DO WHAT YOU WANT)

■

I remember feeling stunned by Jack's letter—as if I'd been propelled toward him, only to be shot down in midflight. It had just been a few weeks since he'd set up housekeeping in Berkeley. Why couldn't he give California more of a chance? Why did he feel so threatened? Even though I knew that a week after Jack's arrival on the Coast, the police had raided the City Lights bookstore and confiscated all the copies of *Howl*, Jack's reaction seemed extreme.*

And what did he mean when he wrote, "Do what you want"? Was this a gentle way of saying he didn't really want me?

*I didn't realize that he was now afraid that Viking would back out of publishing *On the Road*.

Reading the letter many years later, I'm struck by all Jack's angry references to old people, equating them with the cops. Was he feeling the constraints of living with his mother*—something he never would have admitted—and seizing upon an excuse to back out of the arrangement?

Jack's change of plans certainly left me out on a limb—I'd persuaded my parents to accept my departure, given up my apartment, gotten rid of most of my household belongings. And now, I was only moving as far as the residence hotel at the end of my block. I'd always sworn that whatever happened to me, I would never live in the Yorkshire—an end-of-the-line sort of place, filled with Columbia dropouts and alcoholics and people just released from mental hospitals. Fortunately, I hadn't yet given up my job, so if I had to stay in New York and start all over again, I'd be able to do so. But what an anticlimax that would be.

Soon after Jack's letter arrived, there was another crisis. Elise Cowen had been very depressed ever since Allen's departure for Tangiers—she knew it would be at least a year before she'd see him again. With Allen gone, her life seemed to fall apart. That spring she had taken a night job as a typist for TelePrompTer. She began showing up there erratically, even coming in drunk. One night in late June, as soon as she arrived, they told her she was fired. Elise did not react rationally. She sat down at her desk and refused to leave. "I want a reason or explanation," she kept repeating, as if she'd turned into Bartleby the Scrivener. The police carried her out of the premises and summoned her parents to the precinct to pick her up. Two days later, feeling shaken and humiliated, she bought a bus ticket and fled to the Coast.

Elise's departure suddenly cleared up my indecision. Despite my uncertainty about Jack's plans, I promised to join her in San Francisco as soon as I could. We would be roommates and look out for each other there. I'd have my own adventure with or without Jack.

*Gabrielle Kerouac had not taken to Berkeley at all, missed her daughter Nin and her grandson in Florida, hated the climate, and no doubt made Jack constantly aware of her unhappiness.

There was a certain amount of bravado in this new plan, but when I got some good news about my novel at the end of the following week and a more optimistic-sounding postcard from Jack, all my confidence returned.

■

[Postcard from Berkeley, California]
[June 27, 1957]
Dear Joyce, Disregard last letter, I think I exaggerated conditions here in gloomy mood. . . . Go ahead as planned, I'll be with you all the way . . . all the way to Mexico, eventually, I have an idea . . . and you must write novel about Mexico too!

Love
Jack

p.s.
My mother says if she's still here when you arrive SanFran, we will have a nice dinner for you
(she's leaving & I'm staying)

■

It pains me to see that when I answered Jack, I didn't reveal how much his vacillations had upset me. What was the point of that when I was following his dictum—going on this trip because I really wanted to? By now I realized I might get off the bus and find Jack's mood had changed yet again, but at least my mind was made up.

It was nearly a month, though, before I received another letter from him.

■

Dear Jack,

I got both your letter and your card and want to come out
and am coming. I wish I could talk to you. Letters are very un-
satisfactory sometimes—like dropping bottles into the ocean,
and now and then San Francisco seems like the end of the
world. But I love you and want to see you and if you want me
to come out, that makes me very happy. I haven't written you
all week because I've been thinking about all this, and one
thing after another has been popping in New York, so it's been
hard to keep everything straight. But look, Dear, please don't
worry about me. It's not necessary, and I don't want to be one
more thing to bug you. I guess San Francisco's probably like
New York or any other place in the world—every once in a
while you have a great day and the rest of the time you don't
and just keep going.

The only thing is—that now I'll be delayed a bit, probably
three weeks, maybe less. The reason is that Hiram Haydn has
finally offered me a contract for the book, and I've got to stick
around while everything is being straightened out. I'll be getting
some money, probably around $250, which will be a great help
when I come out, because then for a while I can get along on a
part-time job, while I'm working on the rest of the book. (Do you
think there are part-time jobs in the University?) I'm very
excited, still can't believe all this has happened, but it's also a little scarey to be formally committed to finish up now—maybe it
will push me along a little faster, though.

Also, this week—I had a stupid fight with Connie [Robins],
who flipped and evicted me, so I've been running all over the city
looking for a temporary place to stay and living in three different
apartments—it's been awful! I've accumulated a very impressive
collection of keys to places where I'm no longer living. But today
I wound up most anticlimactically in a hotel on 113th Street.
The address is: Yorkshire Residence Hotel, 562 West 113th
Street—send all letters there from now on. Remember when you

said to me—"If you ever want to move, call Henri Cru."* Well, I had to move everything out in a hurry and I was too flipped to remember his name, so I phoned the first moving company I saw in the Village Voice and it turned out to be Henri Cru after all! We had beers in the West End, and he told me about the days when you were at school together, and how you used to steal ice cream when you were a cop in California. I never knew you'd been a cop.

Has Elise gotten in touch with you yet? She left for San Francisco last Saturday very suddenly. She had gotten herself into a jam here and got fed up. She hasn't sent me her address yet. I'm sort of worried about her.

Well, that's a lot for one week, isn't it?

Write soon and tell me how you are and what's happening to you.

Love,
Joyce XXX

P.S. I'd love to go to Mexico!

July 8, 1957

Dear Jack,

Since I wrote you Saturday, everything has cleared up beautifully!

My parents suddenly became angelic over the weekend and are giving me their blessing, a suitcase, and are going to pay my fare to California. So I'll be stinking rich, or almost. Anyway, I won't have to do anything except work on the book and dig San Francisco for two or three months. Isn't that lovely? My agent tells me everything will be settled† by August 1st—

---

*Henri Cru and Jack had met at Horace Mann prep school when Jack spent a year there on a football scholarship. The character Remi Boncoeur in *On the Road* was based upon him. Cru now worked for a Village moving company called The Padded Wagon.
†On the basis of the first fifty pages, Hiram Haydn was buying my novel for Random House and offering me a one-thousand-dollar advance, which seemed like a fortune in those days.

Therefore I guess I'll see you sometime around August 10th or 11th. My parents are insisting I fly, and since they're paying, I will.

I'm very happy and am beginning to believe in good luck. And I'm a little hung-over from pernod with friends last night, but feel great.

Various people seem to have gotten hold of Evergreen No. 2 and are very enthusiastic about the freight-yard piece.* I'm trying to track down a copy now too.

Love,
Joyce

P.S. If by chance, you run into Elise on the hilly streets of San Francisco, you might tell her all this. See you.

[Postcard from Elise Cowen depicting Lombard Street in San Francisco, popularly known as "the crookedest street in the world."]

July 5

Joyce,

Haven't seen this street yet, but most of SF white & in North Beach bay-windowed. Haven't gotten down to Berkeley yet. Jack only goes to The Place only every couple of weeks it seems. Beautiful city especially for what you can see from it. Prices no lower than N.Y., but values brimful—style emphasized, extremes norm. People—much like N.Y. but don't really know yet. A little East Side–sick.

Write.
Love,
Elise

*"October in the Railroad Earth" had just been published in the *Evergreen Review*.

Dear Elise,

Miserable wretch, why don't you write? What's happening to you in the crooked streets?

I'm coming, I'm coming—but at the moment I'm in one of those nervous, gloomy states between letters from Jack. Haven't heard from him since I wrote him I was on my way. My parents are incredible—they keep saying when can we buy the plane ticket for you, do you want a valise, what clothes do you want— they've put the photographs of me back on the wall,* but not the oil portrait. It all makes me feel very disoriented somehow, since parents are not supposed to cooperate.

I got my contract from Random House, a very beautiful piece of paper, and the check for $500 will be forwarded to Frisco— maybe I'll have them send it c/o you, if that's okay.

I've been spending a lot of time in the Cedar since it seems as though almost everybody I know has either disappeared or is dis- appearing or they're sticking it out and becoming somewhat intolerable company. I've met a lot of painters and think they're wonderful, vigorous people, even though very often I don't know what the hell they're talking about. And I've made friends with Fee [Fielding Dawson]† who is indeed very lovely—it's uncanny, isn't it, the way he digs people immediately sometimes? And I like the way he knows exactly what he likes—"That's terrific! That's terrific!" Who have you met in S.F.?

[Sheila's] leaving next week, and I'm going to see her off in Hoboken. Haven't had a chance to see her otherwise yet. Maybe she doesn't particularly want to see me.

Donald doesn't have a job yet, altho' he stands a good chance of getting a terrific one—research for Columbia Psychiatric. He's being both self-absorbed and manic, burning up more little girls.

As I wrote you, I'm living in the Yorkshire. In a little green room with flowered cretonne drapes. I share a sink with a myste-

---

*They took them down when I left home.
†By now I was actually having an affair with him.

rious man named Frank J. Redd, who has six different kinds of mouthwash.

Come on now—write!

Love,
Joyce

July 22, 1957
1418 Clouser St.
Orlando, Fla.

Dear Joyce—

I moved my mother back to Orlando, leaving me with $33, which I think is a big joke in the family, since she wound up around the corner from where we started & everybody comes around every night to laugh— The review copy of On the Road's unread on the shelf,—and now, beyond the bugging stage, I'm becoming enraged so I'm going to Mexico tomorrow on the chance Viking will feed me down there— I saw Elise in Frisco, I was too much for her with drinking gangs behind me— Everything exploded— I was afraid to write to you— But here's your enraged bum— Are you going to Frisco anyway? P'raps you should spend your money on fixing a new pad in the Village, or come down to Mexico & join me after Frisco— Write to me care of here, I'll reply from Mexico City— In the next 6 weeks in Mexico City I want to write by candlelight in a solitary room, think & stare thru the wall— My Buddhist friend Whalen advised me to [do] this noticing I was being *set upon* too much by family obligations— It's what I was going to do anyway, absorb vibrations—

So, sweet Joycey, decide what you wanta do— if you care to join me in Mexico City in September or so, come on down, you can buy a Greyhound ticket straight thru from N.Y. to Mexico City, check your baggage straight through— Lush apartments for $20 a month, I'll be in an $11 hovel myself—

Frisco was too much, but maybe you can dig it & Elise is a little lost, I think— She thinks I'm irresponsible—but No! I'm just sick! crazy! We got a letter from my sister and had to leave or lose the pad— Now I'm broke but conscience-free and ready to do some writing—*

I'll write to you next week from my new address— You got a good advance! In a year we'll both be rich & corrupt!

Jack

P.S. $500 can last you *10* months in Mexico & write all you want

July 26, 1957

Dear Jack,

Yes, yes, I will come to Mexico!

I wish you hadn't been afraid to write me. I know you have to do what you have to do, and that isn't being a bum—don't put yourself down like that. Elise wrote me that you'd left, but her letter was so vague that it sounded as though you were in some terrible trouble and had decided to disappear, and I've spent a sad week, wanting so much to write you not to disappear and not knowing where to write— so that it was just too much to get your letter. I walked out of the hotel with it in my hand, ordered an enormous breakfast that I couldn't eat, and *flew* downtown in the IRT, which I think I imagined as somehow bound for Mexico that minute. Yes, and I bought a learning-Spanish-phonetically-thru-pictures type book and can already say Yo soy muchacha, a sentence which I'm sure will come in very handy eventually. I wish it were September.

It worries me, Jack, to think of you with $33 to your name while Viking's machinery works out a way of feeding you. And I've really got all this money—so would you like some in the meanwhile? Let me know, and I'll send you a money order or whatever.

I got a review copy of ON THE ROAD, read it, and think it's a great, beautiful book. I think you write with the same power

*He planned to do some further work on *Dr. Sax* and then submit it to Viking, which had turned down *Desolation Angels* while Jack was in California. Viking rejected *Dr. Sax* too just before Jack left Mexico City.

and freedom that Dean Moriarty drives a car. Well, it's terrific, and very moving and affirmative. Don't know why, but it made me remember Mark Twain. Ed Stringham has read it too and thinks it "one of the best books since World War II" and is going to write you a long letter and tell you all this, much more coherently than I can.

Saw [Sheila] off to Europe Wednesday on a little white ship not much bigger than a ferry boat, full of waving singing young kids. Everybody smiling and throwing streamers, [Sheila] too, but I didn't know how she felt. It's funny the way you and Allen and Peter came to town this winter and shook us all up. Just think— we had been here all our lives, and now suddenly Elise is in Frisco, [Sheila] in Paris, and I'm going to Mexico—most peculiar. I feel rather friendless in New York at present, miss talking to Elise a lot, especially. She called me collect from San Francisco this week because she needed money and we tried to talk but couldn't hear each other and kept screaming "Wh-a-a-t? Wh-a-a-t." But then I remember walking with you at night through the Brooklyn docks and seeing the white steam rising from the ships against the black sky and how beautiful it was and I'd never seen it before—imagine!—but if I'd walked through it with anyone else, I wouldn't have seen it either, because I wouldn't have felt safe in what my mother would categorically call "a bad neighborhood," I would have been thinking "Where's the subway?" and missed everything. But with you—I felt as though nothing could touch me, and if anything happened, the Hell with it. You don't know what narrow lives girls have, how few real adventures there are for them; misadventures, yes, like abortions and little men following them in subways, but seldom anything like seeing ships at night. So that's why we've all taken off like this, and that's also part of why I love you.

Take care.

Love,
Joyce

P.S. When you write next maybe you could say something about the Mexican climate, whether it ever gets cold, so I'll know what to bring with me. As you've probably gathered by now, I'm incredibly vague about geography.

■

Elise later admitted to me that she'd "flipped out" the night she'd run into Jack in North Beach, which had unfortunately ended with the two of them in bed together. I remember feeling strangely unperturbed by this news. Elise and Jack were the two people I loved most, and both of them had been in deep trouble at the time. Somehow what had happened between them on that drunken night in North Beach seemed no more meaningful than an accident. It was easy enough, I knew, to end up in the wrong bed without quite meaning to, especially if you were lonely. I had discovered that my own brief affair that summer with Fielding Dawson had little effect upon my feelings for Jack.

By the time my letter of July 26 arrived in Orlando, Jack, still under the impression I was planning to join Elise in San Francisco, had arrived in Mexico City. This was his seventh trip there, and it would be his unhappiest. Ever since Jack's first visit in 1951, Mexico had implanted itself in his mind as a kind of Shangri-la, a land of endless kicks, fantastic beauty, and low prices—a destination that held out the promise of providing a solution to all his problems.

But this time, Mexico City seemed immediately unwelcoming. When Jack went to the house on Orizaba Street where he had lived in a rooftop hut and written *Dr. Sax,* he learned that his friend Bill Garver, a drug addict Burroughs had introduced him to, was dead, and no one knew the whereabouts of Esperanza Villanueva, the Mexican prostitute he had once loved, who had inspired him to write *Tristessa.*

Then came the terrifying earthquake of 1957 in which thousands died all around him.

■

Dear Joyce

The giant earthquake was this morning at 3 AM, I woke up
with my bed heaving & I *knew* I wasn't at sea, but in the dark I'd
forgotten where I was except it was in this world & here was the
end of the world— I stayed in bed & went back to sleep, figuring
if my giant 20-foot ceiling was to fall on my bed, *everybody* would
die inside or outside buildings— It was just like that Atlantic
tempest last February, darkness & fury— I could hear sirens wailing & women wailing outdoors but the hush of silence was in my
ears, that is, I recognized that all this living & dying & wrath was
taking place inside the Diamond Silence of Paradise—twice this
year I've had the vision *forced* on me— Well, there wont be
another earthquake like this here for another 50 years so come on
down, I'm waiting for you—

Dont go to silly Frisco— First place, I have this fine
earthquake-proof room for 85c a night for both of us, it's an
Arabic magic room with tiles on the walls & many big round
whorehouse sex-orgy mirrors (it's an old 1710 whorehouse, solid
with marble floors)—we can sleep on the big clean doublebed,
have our private bath (also with 20-foot ceiling & cloistral bas-
relief Mohammedan windows)—it's right downtown, you can
enjoy city life to the hilt then when [we] get tired of our Magian
inwardness Sultan's room we can go off to the country & rent a
cottage with flowerpots in the window—

—Your money will last 5 times longer & in Frisco you
wouldnt be seeing anything *new* & *foreign* & *strange*— Take the
plane to Mexico City (bus too long, almost as expensive too),
then take a cab to my hotel, knock my door, we'll be gay friends
wandering arm-in-arm in Mexico— Also, we'll do our writing &
cash our checks in big American banks & eat hot soup at market
stalls & float on rafts of flowers & dance the rumba in mad joints
with 10c beers— Perhaps you can go to Frisco see Elise *after*
Mexico, & complete your educational tour— But I am lonesome
for yr. friendship & love, so try to come down, lots to talk about,

lots of sleeping & loving, eating & drinking & walking & visiting cathedrals & pyramids & wait till you drink big waterglasses of cold fresh orange juice every morning for 7c !!—& giant T-bone steaks for 85c that you cant finish!—& I'll show you sights most Americans dont know exist here & you can write a big book—

After this I am going back to N.Y., via Florida, perhaps we can go back together—

At first, I thought I wanted to be alone & stare at the walls, but now I realize, after the earthquake, no one can be alone, even one's own body is not "alone," it is a vast aggregate of smaller living units, it is a phantom universe in itself— And maybe I've come to realize this now because in this altitude (8000 ft.) I dont get drunk, & I'm not taking drugs any more (my connections are dead), & I just stare healthily at the interesting world— Come on, we'll be 2 young American writers on a Famous Lark that will be mentioned in our biographies— Write soon as you can, this address, I'll be waiting for your answer—

Jack XXX

■

The need and love Jack finally declared obliterated from my mind any consideration of the consequences of the earthquake. Nor did I take sufficient note of the fact that Jack had written this letter, so different in tone from all the others, during one of the few periods in recent years when he was completely sober. I only knew there suddenly seemed to be a profound change in our relationship. Here were the feelings, the "real" feelings, he had always held back.

Jack's invitation was so irresistible that I gave up my job the day after his letter of June 27th arrived. I had begun to feel very doubtful, in view of Jack's many changes of mind, that I would actually leave New York, so I had just accepted a promotion at Farrar, Straus & Cudahy. Robert Giroux had asked me to be his assistant, which in 1957 seemed a fantastic step up from being a secretary. Now I had to walk into Giroux's office and inform him that instead, I would be flying down to Mexico City to join Jack and to finish my novel. After I gave Mr. Giroux this news, there was a moment of deep, stunned silence, but then he wished me luck. He also said, "Well, be careful."

Naturally, I didn't stop to think about this potential setback to my career, although by now I had decided that since I would have to continue earning my keep, I wanted to become an editor. Young women, however, had few opportunities to rise from the secretarial ranks in the 1950s. I was still a secretary five years later when my first novel was finally published.

■

July 31, 1957

Dear Jack,

Got your letter this morning. Guess this will be hitting you the same time as my first letter, which I sent off c/o your mother and which says I'll be coming in September. BUT—Since you want me to come soon, I'll hurry it up as much as I can and will try to take off around the 20th of August or so—I'll make plane reservations later this week and will let you know the exact date. I'm *terribly* excited! Haven't been able to do much here this morning except stare dumbly into the typewriter, make silly little piles of paper to look as though I'm working, and grin—but called up TWA immediately. Oh, my Spanish is progressing beautifully—I can now say and-or-at-hat, etc., and I remember your word *guapo* (is that how you spell it?). Woke up Monday morning and all the papers in the street said EARTHQUAKE IN MEXICO, I flipped for a minute and then somehow *knew* nothing had happened to you, but I was worried about you wandering around with your thirty-three dollars and maybe no place to stay. The earthquake-proof room sounds terrific—I'd hate to have to go all the way to Mexico City and end up in another Yorkshire Hotel with sick green walls and flowered cretonne curtains, drawers that stick in brokendown maple bureaus—you know, real American quasi-respectable ugliness—UGH!

I'd come down immediately, except that I'm really going to need the two weeks more salary from FSC, since my parents have gone back to being blind and righteous and won't encourage me in any "Mexican escapade"—that's how they talk—and they don't seem to know about anything except dysentery, about which they have a vast and detailed knowledge. My agent says "Mexico demoralizes young writers" and thinks I won't finish the book there; she wants me to go to some little New England resort after all the summer people have gone and pretend I'm Sarah Orne Jewett or someone—I think I'd go out of my mind. It's true enough I do find it hard to settle down to work, but I think I'd have that problem anywhere, and what I want to do is to settle down to doing 3–4 hours a day no matter what—you must be very strict with me, Sweetie, and not let me goof off, which ends up making me guilty and sad. I don't know why, but there's something in me that always says Stop when I'm about to lose myself and really go deeply in when I'm writing; I want to fight this very much now and want to talk to you about that, and about everything really.

I've been looking at paintings a lot, just about starting to see them for the first time in my life, and talking to painters—that's been helping me a little. I've always assumed there was only one reality (mine, of course, where everything had to stay fixed, visible and tangible, or I'd get upset), but I'm beginning to see it as an infinitely diverse thing, where teacups can hold up a shelf somehow. Hell, the minute I start to write or talk about it, I still don't know what I mean. I guess I'll stop here; twenty pages more won't make it clearer.

I love you, and am so happy, so proud that you want me to, and that I'll see you again—I know you said I would in Penn Station, but I couldn't really believe it.

Love,
Joyce

Dear Jack,

Just this minute finished making my plane reservation—so I'll be seeing you Wednesday morning, August 21, at ten o'clock, in Mexico City. That seems just unbelievable to me. All I need now is smallpox, which I'll acquire next week. Then—OFF! Okay?

Will you meet me at the airport, or is that terribly far from the city and complicated? Or should I take a taxi to Hotel Luis Moya? (I've learned just about enough Spanish to communicate with the driver.) Oh, I feel like a tourist and I don't care. Alas, poor Jack what will becoming of your silent wall [staring]?—you'll have to shut me up somehow because if I survive the plane ride, I won't be able to get over it. Do you like planes?* I can't help feeling a bit fatalistic about them, and it's a great temptation to call up people and say, "Well goodbye I mean, *really* goodbye." Very silly. Maybe I'll drink lots of champagne at the airport.

Is there anything you'd like me to do for you while I'm still here, or bring you? I don't know—toothpaste, plaid shirts, carbon paper? Can't quite believe that Mexico City is a city. I'm going to drag my typewriter along, even though it's a most unportable portable.

My parents have been giving me lurid descriptions of Mexico—to which they've never been. You'd be fascinated. Wonderful stories of girls disappearing into white slave markets, people injecting free heroin into you on street corners just for the hell of it—they also tell me that the "Asiatic flu" is sweeping up from South America now and is guaranteed to pass *directly* through Mexico City. I told them it would only affect the wicked people, but that didn't seem to satisfy them. (The odd thing is that all this sounds very much like things they've always said about N.Y.)

I'm too full of everything to be able to say very much more right now (and the office manager is giving me suspicious glances because this letter doesn't look very businesslike). Now there'll be two weeks of washing and ironing, wherein I will curse the fact

*I'd never been on one.

that I was born a woman, and the seeing of friends—I wish there were a few days when I could just sit still, think about what everything means and unravel the summer a bit, but no time, no time. Anyhow, the great thing is that I'll be seeing you and talking to you in just two weeks. I had a dream about you in which you were a huge surreal figure; I could see you while I was reading a letter you wrote me from a place called called Green County, Idaho, where you were staying on a ranch with an old man and a woman who you said were saints, and there you were, striding happily through Idaho, which was lush, green, almost tropical, and I was amazed because I had always thought of Idaho as desert country. (So you see, even in dreams my knowledge of geography is way off.)

Write soon.

Much love,
Joyce

P.S. Much "trade word of mouth" about ON THE ROAD, which is a very healthy thing. Also—on Sunday in the Times, Harvey Breit put it first on his list of Fall novels which were going to make people sit up and take notice.

[Mexico City]
August

Dear Joyce

I'm having an awful case of Asiatic flu, been in my gloomy room alone for 3 days trying to sweat it out in my sleeping bag with hot toddies and pills— I thought I was going to die there for awhile when I began shaking violently from fever— I had to get up & go out & sip soup—& try to cash checks at uncooperative American Embassy ("Protection Department" indeed)— "It's against regulations" they tell me dead on my feet & in need of medicine—How I made it I dont know, but I do know I cant get any writing done this trip in Mexico, just a round of bad luck has hexed my visit— God know what'll happen next— As soon as I can walk without feeling weak I'm taking a bus back

to Florida to my home & my room— My neck is swollen up like
a bejowled millionaire's— As soon as I'm home I'll write to
you again and we can decide where we'll meet— For one thing,
I'll be coming to N.Y. this Fall undoubtedly (business will crop
up)— I don't want you to be confused, this latest "change of
mind" I cant help, I'm sick & need care— Will you write to me
at Clouser St?

Jack

[Excerpts from a letter from Elise Cowen]
[San Francisco]
[early August 1957]

Dear Joyce,

The days fly by . . . Just realized this morning that you'll be
leaving for Mex. shortly after this reaches you. What great happy
fears and excitement you must be feeling now. . . . Well Rejoyce,
have a beautiful celebration & lovetime. Give my embarrassed
hello to Jack.

Oh, Don Allen said that William Hogan of the S.F. Chronicle
would like a "statement" (?) about On the Road from Jack . . . some
personal material.

N.Y. is going to be that old tree falling in the empty forest now.

Love,
Elise

August 13, 1957

Dear Jack,

Don't know whether you're in Florida by now or still in Mexico City, but hope you're feeling much better. The flu sounds like
a terrible thing. Since I never read the papers, I thought it was
just one of my mother's inventions and now feel awful about
being so flip about it in my letter to you before I heard you had it.
Did you get my special delivery? You didn't answer, and I hope
that means you were able to get the money and someone to take

care of you. I really would have come right down—I did hate to think of you alone in that room.

Well, I shall sit tight now in the Yorkshire until I hear from you. I cashed in my plane ticket without any trouble, and I'd gotten everything washed and ironed, but that's all to the good. And I'm not a bit confused, don't worry about that—just get well. It will make me very happy to see you in New York—or anywhere. I just wish you'd find some place in the world where there's some comfort for you and where whatever demon it is that pursues you from city to city can't find you.

Perhaps, if we're going to meet in New York, I ought to look for an apartment—a cheap, leaseless one. My job ends the end of next week and I'll be home all day writing, and I don't much dig this little green room (don't think you would either). Cheap pads in the Village, I'm afraid, seem to be a nostalgic myth these days—people are paying 90 dollars for closet with fireplace—but there are other parts of the city. What do you think? On the other hand, if you want me to meet you in Topeka, Laredo, New Orleans, etc.—I will pack up and go. Even though I haven't taken off, traveling seems much less scary to me. I've somehow lost my feeling of desperate rootedness and also my devotion to possessions, like every last one of my 300 books. At any rate, I'm back on the novel again, so don't much care where I am.

Take care of yourself, Jack. Drink lots of orange juice. And if you get bored and blue and want company, I'll hop a bus and come visit you, if you'd like that. You'd like New York tonight—it's sharp and cool, the summer shifting gears already—jazz in Central Park, Mozart in Washington Square, and signs all over saying New York is a Summer Festival, which somehow it is now and then. Very demoralizing—I've run away from the typewriter three times tonight to see what's in the street. Write soon.

Love,
Joyce

P.S. Better write me now c/o Yorkshire Hotel, 562 West 113th.

■

I seem to have rallied quickly after this latest setback. New York seemed more and more alluring. Although I was still living on the Upper West Side in the Yorkshire Hotel, I was spending more and more time in the downtown world I had discovered, where each night in the increasingly crowded Cedar fascinating new people seemed to be turning up. In fact, there was a remarkable convergence in New York City that summer of young avant-garde painters, writers, actors, dancers, jazz musicians, as if a signal had gone off all over America, heralding an enormous shift in the culture. It was not the moment to be in Mexico. Although I wouldn't admit it to Jack or even to myself, it would have been hard to tear myself away.

■

[Orlando, Florida]
Sunday Aug 18 '57

Dear Joyce—

I barely got home with high fever and unable to walk, which I've since sweated out in the endless heatwave of Florida August— It wasn't Asiatic Grippe but some kind of Streptococcus infection that wouldn't have amounted to much except I was dehydrated from not drinking water in Mexico (says my old neighbor doctor)— Anyway, Mexico didn't seem to want me this time and drove me right out.

Well, Joyce, since you have writing to do, you should do just that now, establish yourself wherever you like and start working, and I'll come up to see you as soon as Viking sends me more money— I already asked them if they needed any "personal appearances"— I'd sure like to be in N.Y. when ROAD comes out! Unless you'd like to ship me $30 and I could take a bus & come stay with you a month— During that month I'll surely collect $$ on *something,* perhaps the BEAT GENERATION article for Sat. Review, which I just sent in— I'd like that, Autumn in New York!

Even the Yorkshire Green Room sounds good to me—I could take long systematic walks every day during your writing hours—

It'd be pleasant to see Lucien, Cessa & Helen Eliot [sic] again, or go to the 5-Spot with you— If you really have the money, and you were going to send me some in Mexico, go ahead, send it, and I'll be up—I can easily pay it back this Fall— It's so hot in Florida now I dont do any writing anyway.

Someday you'll see Mexico, right now I just couldn't sweat it out sick and alone—it might very well have removed you so far from the concerns of your present novel as to "demoralize" you in a way. As to Frisco, that would have been a waste of money. Save your money for writing time, then when rich go to Paris.

Well, let me know what you're going to do—all I can do now is wait around.

As ever,
Jack

August 21, 1957

Dear Jack,

Came home from the office (my last week) about ten minutes ago and got your letter. Of course, I'll send you a check—here it is, as a matter of fact. I'm so glad you're okay now—I began to be worried, hearing more and more flu details, and just this morning in the office, the special delivery letter I sent you came back with an ominous ADDRESS UNKNOWN on it. . . .

As for the little green room, etc.—I've been looking around for another place and maybe I'll have found something by the time you arrive even. If not, I think it will work out all right— for one thing, I have many 9–5 employed friends living in this neighborhood, and I can certainly find a daytime apart-ment to write in à la studio if need be. Anyhow, although it's a bit awkward, you can cook in the Yorkshire—which should save us some money. Well, none of this is worth worrying about, certainly.

I think I'm going to end up having lots of money, relatively speaking, because FSC is going to write a letter to the Unemploy-ment people saying I've been laid off and then I'll be able to collect $35 a week for 6 months or something—so I'll be rich, won't have to touch most of the Random House money, can save it for Paris, or wherever.

I've met a friend of yours, Bob Creeley,* who is in NY this week, like him a lot—which made me miss you all the more somehow. Maybe he'll still be here by the time you arrive because he seems to be accident prone and his car's been impounded.

Elise sends me a message for you from Donald Allen to the effect that William Hogan would like a "statement" from you about ON THE ROAD, your life, etc. because he's going to review the book.

I think it's fine that you'll be back in town when the book comes out—I think it's fine that you'll be *back!* Let me know what bus you're taking—Shall I meet you at the bus stop, even if dead of night? I'd like to. I've seen so many departures lately, it would cheer me up to see one arrival. Come quick.

Love,
Joyce

Hope you don't have check-cashing trouble in Florida. SOS if so & I'll cancel and send money order—but no cash on hand today—all in bank.

August 21, 1957

Dear Jack,

This is letter No. 2, which must seem a bit strange—but I've fallen into an apartment! It's perfect, very reasonable and well situated—68th Street off Central Park (15 minutes away from practically everything), 2 rooms, good sized and separate (so you won't have to take any walks you don't really want), kitchen with kitchen sink, thank Heaven, etc. It's a sublet from the itinerant

---

*A number of my Black Mountain friends had studied with the poet Robert Creeley. He was the editor of the *Black Mountain Review*.

mother* of a friend of mine, and I can have it from 2–6 months, no lease or anything, and no need to buy furniture or household goods. (The mother is a very sweet, muddled, "bohemian" lady— I told her I wouldn't be alone, and she said of course she understood and thought it was fine, so there won't be any of *that* nonsense.) Besides all this—it's really a very cosy place, not a bit gloomy—I remember being enchanted with it when I was 13 and Mrs. Baker said, Would you like something to drink? and offered me wine.

This is a great relief to me, because although you said the green room didn't sound too bad, I don't like it at all—it embarrasses me living in a place that looks like it's simply given up. I haven't been in it very much since I moved in, and don't think I'd like writing in it for hours and hours each day. Anyway, the apartment will be available Sept. 3, so if you come before that we won't be at the Yorkshire for more than a week—this is a big happy move for me, you realize, shaking Columbia for the first time.

So—we'll be broke but comfortable on 68th Street. I'll make steak and write and learn to light the oven, and we'll listen to jazz (I have a Jai and Kai record now). Maybe you'll want to write—I understand the apartment is very very quiet, although there are jazz musicians up and down the block and ex-Ziegfield follies girls in the house with dyed red hair at 75, but maybe they sleep all day. And we'll get flu injections to protect us from the real flu.

What think you?

Love,
Joyce

P.S. I've taken it!

---

*I had gone to high school with Elsie Baker's daughter Joan Baker Prochnik, a beautiful dancer, who helped me find an apartment in the East Village the following December.

Dear Joyce

Just received your letter and it came just when I felt better
again, and it made me so glad to see the check and hear about
"our" apartment, what a good time we can have in there September! . . . And dont worry about money I'll get some and I'll pay
you back too. What I'll do then, is stay home another week and
see that I dont have a relapse, and leave for NY around Sept. 3 so
I can get in the day of my publication (get into N.Y. and look at
Charles Poore's column) (he gave me a tremendous review in
1950). —So, also, you'll be in that new pad when I get in and I'll
go straight there. Meanwhile I got a letter from Peter and Allen
in Venice, TIME wants to interview Allen and me, they had
Allen fly to Rome so they might conceivably have ME fly to
N.Y., so that's another thing I'll be waiting for all next week then
I could have your check intact to give back to you. I'm writing to
TIME today telling them where I am and that I'm broke. —Say, I
wonder if you could do me a favor: call up Viking Press, ask for
Pat MacManus* of publicity, tell her Jack K. is wondering if she
got the article ABOUT THE BEAT GEN. in the mail and what
she did with it: tell her it's the only statement I ever made about
the Beat Generation, and is the only statement ever made by the
originator of the idea (3 or 4 people have already written about it)
and that tho my article may seem deceptively light-headed it
really is the score (immense historical forces carefully considered
and the "beat generation" carefully placed therein)— Otherwise
there'll be all these imposters having their say-so about the Beat
Generation, all except the originator of the term and the idea,
which is silly. The article will be understood a little later than
now because it has a profound basis. (I compared beatness to the
Second Religiousness prophesied by Spengler, an idea that might

---

*Pat MacManus proved to be Jack's staunchest supporter at Viking. She was often trou-
bled by the effect her well-orchestrated publicity campaign seemed to be having upon
him.

not go over in Sat. Review of Lit. or Harpo's Bazaar, with their contempt for "rock and rollers" but it's TRUE.)

If TIME doesnt send me a ticket, I'll cash yr. check at my sister's bank and come up anyhow. Meanwhile send me the new address and phone number. Just wait at the pad for me, I'll let you know app. when I'll be in, just have a drink ready to pour, we're gonna have a ball.

I got a message from Elise about Frisco newspaperman wants a letter from me, but that's all I heard, message thru Allen G. in Venice. But she must be okay. Oops, that was thru you.

Your parents oughta be pleased you're staying in NY. By the way, are they going to let you publish under yr. real name? I hope so. Your reputation will be no more lurid than Virginia Woolf's, after all.

Oh, please write and tell me in detail how and where you met Bob Creeley and what happened and what he said [about] what he's going to do. You know, he's a mysterious figure and everyone was wondering where he was. Publishes Black Mtn. Review. Is it out yet? the new issue with me in it?

Jai and Kai record, ah, I can hardly wait till I get "home"— We'll have a great time and I always feel better in the Fall but I feel extry fine now because I was so sick. I dont think I'll catch flu or that you'll catch anything from me. I feel too good now. —Well, write to me right away, and I'll answer right back. I can hardly wait till I have you in my arms.

Jack

Monday, [August 26]

Dear Jack,

Your letter just arrived. I'm writing this now (10 A.M.), taking care of small seven-year-old boy madly rocking in my rocking chair with OZ books, chewing-gum, MIGHTY MOUSE comics, and "I Ride an Old Paint" on the phonograph. —I'm to take him to the Museum of Natural History to see all the dinosaurs and he's impatient, says "Hurry up, Joy-is."

The address will be: c/o Elsie Baker, 65 West 68th Street (TRafalgar 7-8771—I *think*, but worse comes to worse this name is in the phone book, which I don't have here). I'll be waiting for you on September 5th then—right?—with a very large gin and tonic or something and terribly excited listening for you to come up the stairs (there are four flights of them—it's, in a sense, the penthouse!)

It would be lovely if TIME gave you a free plane ride, much pleasanter and faster than the bus too. But, however it works out, *don't* worry abut the $30—I seem to be quite adequately supplied with money, much to my amazement.

Ed Stringham wants me to tell you that he'd like to give a party for you, if you'd like that (he *never* gives parties—but he seems to be quite serious about this).

How I met Bob Creeley: He is a friend of friends of mine who are painters from Black Mountain and was in the Cedar Bar one night last week . . . I knew it was him the minute I saw him from the way he'd been described*—he looks straight out of Nathaniel Hawthorne to me, somehow. He seems to have a reputation in these parts for causing trouble, all kinds of fights . . . but he was very quiet, self-contained, stared at me solemnly and asked me most kindly what I wrote about, told me I was "a little blonde girl," and suggested much later that we "take a walk"—but we didn't (I had the feeling that somehow he was joking all the time, but on the other hand if you took him seriously he'd go along with you as far as you'd let him—do you know what I mean?). He is pretty damn mysterious. He spoke a lot of you, said he was "proud to consider myself Jack Kerouac's friend," kept talking about some fight you'd rescued him from in Frisco. Did you know that he lives in Albuquerque? He has a job there teaching little boys French and American History and is married (happily, it seems). I think he's left town by now—too bad he won't be here when you come. He didn't mention the Black Mountain Review—I don't think it's out yet.

---

*A romantically gaunt figure dressed in black, with an eye patch.

I'm enclosing the dull and uninspired review of the NEW DIRECTIONS ANTHOLOGY* from the Sunday Trib. Reviews like this make me mad! All the man says is, "Oh dear me, how much violence they all express!" without committing himself about how much violence *he* feels there is in the world, so it reduces this book to a literary curiosity—and he makes no attempt to see beyond the "violence and anger."

I just called Viking and spoke to Pat MacManus. The article came 10 days ago when she was on vacation, and her assistant sent it to Harper's (unlikely place, I should think), but it came back, and now she's sent it out again to the Saturday Review. She promised to write you a letter about it tomorrow.

Well, Sweetie, Michael [Cook] (the seven-year-old) is just about ready to burst and I don't blame him—this room is very small and he likes to run and shinny up lampposts and he's read all his comics—so it's time to go.

I've felt most happy and peaceful ever since you wrote you were coming—I've been working on the book. And now there's packing to do, all those 300 books are still with me and now there are a few more. I'll ask Henri Cru to help me move—since he said I should the last time. By the time you arrive, I'll be all moved in, unpacked, arranged—so the timing is perfect. Since I wrote you last, I've acquired another record, Lee Wiley—very beautiful.

See you a week from Thursday!

Love,
Joyce
xxx

Looking forward to your *last* letter.

P.S. Viking is sending out lovely ads for *On the Road* to people in the trade—quotes from the book on postcards, with picture of the jacket. Two different ones. I've saved them for you.

*Jack was one of the contributors.

[Orlando, Florida]
[end of August, 1957]

Dear Joyce

Just a note . . . I had to spend some of your money on food, so
have to wait till Wednesday 4th to leave, when my mother gets
social security check, so will be in Friday 6th and take the subway
to 65 West 68th . . . As you can see, I was truly broke. After this
trip, no more. Till then, Jack.

■

The trips I didn't take in the summer of 1957 have always
haunted me. They would have tested me profoundly, altered the
future course of my life in unknown ways. I still regret that I couldn't
move faster than Jack Kerouac could change his mind, that I never
saw Jack's Mexico, never underwent the "educational" experience
he offered—even with all its risks.

I see myself getting off the plane in Mexico City, finding my
way to the Luis Moya hotel, the one building left standing in a
street of rubble. Sometimes Jack's right there waiting for me; he
gets up from the bed and holds out his arms as I walk into the room
with the enormous mirrors. Sometimes he's been gone for days and
the leering proprietor has no idea when he'll be back—"Borracho,"
he says. "Muy borracho." "Non comprende," I answer, opening my
suitcase to get out my Spanish-English dictionary. . . .

Sometimes Jack and I look at cathedrals and Orozcos and eat
those amazing steak dinners I insist on paying for; we take a bus out
to the countryside and rent a thick-walled cottage the color of a
flowerpot, where each day we peacefully work on our books and
make love. And then it's September and On the Road is published,
but Jack knows he'll be happiest just the way we are and wisely
decides not to go up to New York. Bulging envelopes stuffed with
reviews, articles, checks, fantastic offers of all kinds, keep arriving
in the mail, but the brouhaha seems very far away. Back in the
States everyone wonders about this mysterious writer Kerouac who

has chosen to bury himself in a small Mexican village at the very time the world is clamoring to get a look at him. . . .

But here's a more realistic scenario: As the weeks pass in our quiet cottage, Jack's mood unaccountably darkens. He talks about feeling bored and gets dangerously silent; soon he's going out to the local bars, stumbling home with drunken strangers who scare me. When his publisher insists that he has to come to New York, he promises to be gone only a few weeks—how can he deprive himself of the experience of being the most famous writer in America? But he forgets to return. When I walk alone through the village, people stare at me and call me la Gringa; at night teenage boys rattle the door and knock on my windows. I wait for Jack until almost all my money is gone. Then I hitchhike back to New York and write an entirely different novel.

I saw San Francisco for the first time in the early 1970s. Passing the Greyhound bus terminal one day, I felt compelled to go inside. It was a gray-brown place, smaller than I'd expected, with poor people and derelicts waiting on wooden benches. Obviously it had never been renovated; it would have looked much the same, I thought, in the summer of '57. I walked over to the arrival gates and found the one marked New York—the gate I would have walked through.

I have never been to Mexico City.

Part III

.

September-November,
1957

ON LABOR DAY, MONDAY, SEPTEMBER 2, Jack rang the doorbell of my new brownstone apartment on West Sixty-eighth Street. At midnight we went out and got the *New York Times* and found the extraordinary review of *On the Road* by Gilbert Millstein that immediately established Jack as the avatar of the Beat Generation and one of the most important American writers since Ernest Hemingway. For once, Jack had had some phenomenal luck. Millstein, who had been keenly interested in the Beats ever since John Clellon Holmes's prophetic 1952 article "This Is the Beat Generation," happened to be substituting that day for the *Times'* regular reviewer Charles Poore, a conservative gentleman who was away on vacation. Although Poore had admired *The Town and the City*, Jack would not have become famous overnight if he had reviewed *On the Road*.

Since *Times* reviews had awesome power, Millstein's response to Jack's book stirred up an instant media blitz. This fellow Kerouac was obviously good copy, with his shocking ideas about sex and drugs that threatened the American way of life. Jack was besieged with requests for interviews—including appearances on some of the first talk shows on TV, an unprecedented kind of exposure for a writer.

But Jack had dreamed of having a *literary* success. He had never wanted to become the spokesman for a generation, despite his proprietary feelings about originating the whole concept of Beat. That was a role Allen Ginsberg could have played brilliantly in the fall of 1957—if he had been around to share the spotlight instead of being in Paris.

Apart from a few reviews, much of the critical attention *On the Road* received was hostile and humiliating. As Gertrude Stein once astutely pointed out in her essay on Picasso, anything truly new and innovative in art is initially considered ugly. Just as Jackson Pollock's ground-breaking paintings had been described as work that could have been done by a chimpanzee, Jack's true literary achievement—his breakthrough into spontaneous prose—was dismissed by Truman Capote as "typewriting" and either overlooked or cruelly derided by critics from the literary establishment like Norman Podhoretz, who accused Jack of wanting to "replace civilization by the street gang." According to the *Hudson Review*, Jack wrote like "a slob running a temperature"; the *Herald-Tribune* found him "infantile," and Charles Poore, far less enthusiastic than Millstein, wrote off the Beat Generation as a "sideshow of freaks" in the Sunday *Times*. By October, with columnist Herb Caen's invention of the term *beatnik*, the Beat Generation had been thoroughly trivialized by the mass media and at the same time made available for easy, empty imitation, a phenomenon that Jack found profoundly disturbing.

He coped with his bewildering notoriety by drinking—cheap wine, champagne, cocktails, whatever he could get. I still naively did not think of him as an alcoholic—he just seemed to be going through a particularly difficult time. But I knew he was in danger. On the night of a party Gilbert Millstein gave in Jack's honor, the day after his humiliating appearance on the talk show *Night Beat*, when he drunkenly told the American public he was waiting for God to show him His face, Jack felt too fearful and depressed to leave the apartment. He told his friend John Clellon Holmes,*

---

*Jack always knew that he could count on Holmes's support and good sense, even though he had never quite forgiven Holmes for writing about the Beat Generation before he did, in Holmes's *New York Times* article "This Is the Beat Generation" and the novel *Go,* both published in 1952.

who came to see him that night, "I don't know who I am anymore."

Toward the end of September, Jack almost proposed to me during a weekend away from the stresses of fame in Lucien Carr's old farmhouse in upstate New York. Before Jack and Lucien began an all-night session of heavy drinking, we had a memorable dinner featuring the first apple pie I had ever made, which Jack promptly christened "Ecstasy Pie." "I know we should just stay up here and get married," he said to me after a walk in the woods the following day. I said, "I know that, too," and we left it at that.

The next weekend we returned to Lucien's house. This time the plan was that we would leave Jack alone up there for a week. He still believed solitude would help him heal himself—it had worked for him in the past, he insisted, forgetting how close he'd come to cracking up on Desolation Peak. The experiment lasted one day— Jack thumbed a ride with a truck driver who brought him back to New York very embarrassed and disappointed with himself. He abruptly departed for his mother's house in Orlando, buying eight White Castle hamburgers to eat on the train (he had not lost his old thrifty habits). Although I was sad to see him go, I knew how badly he needed to escape for a while into the only remaining vestige of his old life.

In New York, I continued to work on my novel. It always seemed physically possible to finish it within a six-month period, but I would not deliver the completed manuscript to Hiram Haydn until 1961. My chaotic but heady existence kept pulling me away from it. In addition to Jack, there were the continuing distractions of the downtown art world and the Cedar Tavern.

I was becoming very friendly with the first interracial couple I had ever known—the young black poet LeRoi Jones, who after reading *Howl* had written to Allen Ginsberg on toilet paper asking "Are you sincere?," and his wife Hettie, who had grown up in a middle-class Jewish household on Long Island and was working at *Partisan Review*. Since there was so much exciting new writing around and no place to publish it, the Joneses talked about starting

a literary magazine of their own, even if it had to be typed on sten-
cils by Hettie and mimeographed rather than printed.*

During one of my downtown excursions, I was surprised to run
into an acquaintance from Hunter High School—Diane di Prima,
who had edited Hunter's literary magazine and was now living in a
tenement on Houston Street with her baby daughter and writing
fiercely funny poems as sexually frank as the ones written by men.
None of the other women I met seemed to be writing, or at least
they didn't talk about it. At the coffee-shop poetry readings I
began going to, all the avant-garde readers, with the exception of
Diane, were men. I wouldn't have dreamed of standing up to read
a chapter of my "college novel," which felt less and less relevant to
the cultural revolution that seemed to be flourishing all around me,
although in spirit, I knew it was Beat. Except for Jack's continued
encouragement, I felt very alone with my work. In the world of the
defiantly unpublished male writers I was meeting, the validation of
my contract with a "square" publisher didn't seem to count. In fact,
it made me feel like an outsider.

■

Monday
[mid-September 1957]

Dear Elise,

Very, very glad to get your letter—never actually *got* it, but it
was read to me over the phone by Don [Cook] who fucked up
and mislaid it for a couple of days. Otherwise I would have
answered sooner. Now, please write the descriptive letter you
promised.

Of course, I still love you—whatever happened in Frisco (and
I think you've exaggerated that anyway). As for Jack—he speaks
of you as "great Elise" with nothing but fondness and feels badly

*A year later they started *Yugen*, a little magazine with two hundred readers and a big
impact. Kerouac, Ginsberg, Corso, Diane di Prima, Gilbert Sorrentino, Robert Creeley,
Barbara Guest, Charles Olson, and Frank O'Hara were among the writers Hettie and
LeRoi published.

about scaring you. Jack is here in town now, has been for 2½ weeks—he may leave tomorrow, but may stay another week—the plans keep changing. All the publicity doings in connection with ON THE ROAD bugged him quite a bit. There've been a round of parties with vast phalanxes of hand-shaking people who think the Beat Generation is so-o-o fascinating, isn't it?—everyone pours drinks down him trying to make him live up to the book—and there are lots of eager little girls everywhere who say, "ooh, let's go to my house for a party" at four o'clock in the morning (they are my pet dislike and I've developed quite a sharp tongue, I'm afraid: "Look sister, there isn't going to be any party," etc., etc.) Also we've met a geeklike radio announcer, an AA member with no insides of his own left who gets his kicks from watching other people, gives Jack goof balls and makes him talk into a tape-recorder— *Him* I would like to murder! Nice people here and there too, but less colorful. All this has destroyed my lovely fantasies about the birth of my own monster—it'll just be nice to get it over with. Aside from this nonsense—it's been great seeing Jack again. I dig ironing his shirts, cooking for him, etc. It's funny—it's not at all romantic anymore, but it doesn't matter—I love him, don't mind playing Mama, since that's what he seems to want me to be. I may go down to see him in Orlando—I've gotten kind of a left-handed backwards invitation (his mother seems to want me to come?). There's no doubt in my mind anymore that Mama is the villain in the true classic Freudian sense.

Love,
Jerce

■

What did I mean by the cryptic "It's not at all romantic anymore"? I guess I was attempting to make the best of my uncomfortable new role as the woman who desperately tried to take care of Jack Kerouac, a responsibility I often felt too young for. Of course I would never have admitted to anyone, not even Elise, that Jack and I were now making love much less frequently than his avid fans would have imagined due to his increasingly heavy drinking. I wondered if what I was experiencing with Jack was anything like marriage, since at times it was almost like having a job.

As for my discovery that I could "dig" housework, which I read now with a wince, I did, in all honesty, find unexpected comfort in everyday tasks. Within the maelstrom of Jack's fame, you could ground yourself for a moment or two by ironing a shirt or cooking a meal. Whatever was normal had come to seem exotic.

One day that fall I bought a notebook in which I planned to begin keeping a journal, but I only wrote one entry:

> At five o'clock in the morning of these endless nights a kind of panic comes over me. . . . I do not know why this is. When I was younger and had to be home on time to find my father getting out of bed to peer at his watch with a flashlight, I wanted to stay up forever and see the dawn and have 6AM coffee in cafeterias with lean, sharp-faced boys in corduroy jackets and walk through the streets of the city and museums and collapse exhausted on someone's couch in a room where six people lie on the rug as if slain . . . but now I insist in tones of outrage that *it is time to go home* even though I do not really want to go there and will probably not be able to sleep—but have only chosen sounds to make, which mean "Look at me. Let me know that you know I'm here."

■

September 16, 1957

Chère [Sheila],

Il me fait très heureuse à recevoir ta lettre "round-robin" et j'espére que tout va bien et que ta française est meilleur que la mienne which has tout à fait flown.

At this moment, I am sitting in my new sublet apartment, 65 West 68th Street (my most swanky address to date!) and M. Kerouac is fast asleep in the next room—not even the typewriter disturbs him. He came to town Sept. 6 the day after ON THE ROAD was published, presumably to stay for a month—but he may go back to Orlando in the next day or so, maybe not. After

the first frenzied week we have been trying to live quietly with
the receiver off the hook most of the day. He sleeps, broods, eats,
stands on his head—I cook, clean, work on my novel—and I *like*
it! Rather—I love him. ON THE ROAD is a great success, looks
like a best-seller already—3 editions sold out so far, may be a
movie, a musical, etc. But sometimes I think people are really out
to kill him—like whispering "doesn't he drink too much?" and
then *pouring* drinks down him, or saying "oh you must meet so-
and-so" who turns out to be boring, empty and vicious—and
he's so innocent, can't play it like a game, but tries to like
everybody and worries about whether or not they really like him
and if they'll be hurt if he doesn't show up at their parties. So
maybe he's better off getting away from New York now—when he
first arrived, he was thinking of living here. In a left-handed,
backwards way, he's invited me to visit him in Orlando "if you
want" —maybe I will.

Have the boys [Ginsberg and Orlovsky] arrived yet? Have you
met Burroughs, [Allen] Anson? Impressions, please—I think you
have a great chattering cockeyed charming style, really! Has poor
Gregory [Corso] recovered his letters? He seems to be incredibly
accident prone. Give him, Allen and Peter my love. What do
you hear from Elise? Jack saw her in Frisco, said she seemed lost. I
think it's a bad place for her and write her saying Why the Hell
don't you come back?, which is maybe why she doesn't write me.
I miss her and you—I had really come to like you enormously all
over again by the time you left. Iris [Michaels]* and I practically
wept as the ship sailed away—everything that happens seems to
be irrevocable lately—I've lost the feeling of dichotomy between
me and the adult world somehow. Well . . . maybe I'll see you in
Paris. I feel as though I'm just treading water now in NY for the
next three months until the book is finished—have no idea what
I'll do then.

Love and write soon,
Joyce

*Another Barnard classmate.

October 14, 1957

Dear Jerce—sweetheart—did you go out with Henri & Bob to
celebrate Bold Ruler's victory in the 7th at Belmont? — I've just
used all my penny postcards answering all my fan letters— Please
lend me Al Hendricks POST & others that I forgot in packing,
I'll send them back. . . . my mother doesn't believe anything. . . .
send reviews with mail— I slept & slept & felt GREAT—raring
to write but no typewriter . . . play in my mind burning . . . My
mother & I decided to move back to L.I. before Spring, so I'll see
you all the time—WRITE!

                                                              Jack

                                                    [mid-October]
                                                    Saturday

Dear Jack,

Have you eaten your eight hamburgers and are you sitting
under an orange tree with your orange cat while pea soup is cooking for you? I am eating pea soup in New York, the radio keeps
playing "Chicago," and I miss you very much.

These two letters came for you today from Allen. Also,
everybody has telephoned: Joe Lustig, Howard [Schulman], Pat
[MacManus], Stringham, etc. No one really believes you've gone.
Young would-be hipsters from Columbia wander through the
Village looking for you in bars. Leo [Garen] is going to write you
a long letter and will send you those rolls of paper. Pat says
Viking seems terribly quiet without you. You left your toothbrush
here as well as your navy blue polo shirt and an envelope full of
clippings (shall I send any of this on to you?). Joe Lustig is still
frantic to arrange readings of everything. He is going to write to
Allen in Paris about the possibility of a reading in late Spring.
The Post interview didn't appear today; when it does next week,
I'll send it to you. Lucien and Cessa were worried that there
might be something in it about Lucien and when they couldn't

reach you here on Wednesday, called Pat who checked up on it for them—but the Post wasn't going to say anything anyway.

How was the trainride? I was kind of worried about that fancy pill Bob Donlin gave you. Did you get to see Milwaukee win? I'm sorry I was so flippy that last day, but everything began to get too loud and too bright somehow, and if I said some bitter words, please forget them. The Hell with the brunettes of the world!* The truth is that I love you—even more now that I've come to know you better—and that makes me happy. Did you know how happy I was last month? And I don't love you just because of the times we have sex but because of the whole totality of you, which is your eating eggs in the morning and listening to the radio and shouting on the stairs, drunk at four o'clock in the morning. I even love you when you're philandering after brunettes. Why all this is as it is—I don't know. I guess if I believe in anything, I believe in the inexplicable. When shall we meet again? If you want me, ask for me.

I am definitely trying to get into Yaddo† for three weeks or so. Don't feel much like hanging around the city and being meaninglessly distracted. Meanwhile, I shall live strictly and write as much as I can. Leo will probably be traveling South in another month and he says he'll give me a lift . . . would you still like that?

My agent has gotten some English publisher vaguely interested in giving me an option for the book, so maybe I'll get a little more money now, which would be lovely.

I'm enclosing a review from the Post which keeps mentioning ON THE ROAD and tries to set up various literary relationships, as you will see—thought it might interest you. Edward [Stringham] tells me that a friend of his in Queens College is teaching it in her English course as "a contemporary novel."

---

*At a party we'd recently gone to, Jack had paid a lot of admiring attention to Helen Weaver, who was looking especially glamorous that night in a red flapper dress. Unknown to me, later in October he would write her, asking to see her again in New York after receiving a package of cigars from her in the mail.
†An artists' colony in Saratoga.

Hope you've found some peace in Florida. New York continues its empty, destructive whirl. Give my regards to your mother. Write soon!

Love,
Jerce

■

I will never forget the eight White Castle hamburgers Jack bought on the day of his departure for Orlando, but I have no precise recollection of the "bitter words" I alluded to in the previous letter. Probably I was expressing my feelings not only about Helen Weaver, but about the whole parade of predatory women who had invaded our life after the publication of *On the Road*. They all seemed to feel entitled to their own piece of Jack and were shameless about proclaiming their intentions. "You're twenty-two, I'm twenty-nine," one of them said to me at a party. "I've got to fuck him now." With Jack as the new apostle of total freedom, any behavior must have seemed permissible.

Some women even followed us home. I remember the combined humiliation and satisfaction of having to throw one of them out—"This is my apartment and you have to leave it—NOW!" Jack, more and more often helplessly drunk, delegated the onerous task of getting rid of his surplus of female admirers to me (a role he would later have his mother take over). Yet of course he was flattered, attracted, immensely susceptible.* Women who wouldn't have been seen with him when he was down and out were flinging themselves at him now. All these new sexual opportunities were like money—part of the spoils of fame.

There is a school of recent Kerouac biography that goes to great—even unconscionable—lengths to "prove," mostly through willful distortion, that Jack was gay. Although I was aware of the intensity of Jack's psychic connections to his male friends, the

---

*"Bway producers bring beautiful models [to] sit on edge of my (girl's) bed, ugh, wanted to make it so much with so many," Jack wrote Neal Cassady when he was back in Florida.

thought that he was homosexual never occurred to me when I was with him (nor did it, for that matter, to other women who had sustained sexual relationships with Kerouac, such as his first wife Edie Parker, Carolyn Cassady [Neal's wife], or Helen Weaver). Indeed, in my own experience, the problem seemed to be Jack's great, insatiable appetite for women, despite his occasional protestations that he wanted to live like a monk.

I was always aware that Jack loved women not only for their bodies but for the stories that came into being as they interacted with him—they were part of his "road," the infinite range of experience that always had to remain open to fuel his work.

Even back then I could understand this, since I only seemed able to fall in love with men who seemed a little larger than life— difficult men like Donald Cook, whom I had turned into a major character in my novel now that everything was over. Dark and exotic women like Allene Lee and Esperanza Villanueva, who inspired *The Subterraneans* and *Tristessa*, had served as Jack's muses. I wondered whether Jack would ever put me in a book, or whether he'd consider me too normal and blond and undramatic. I didn't want to think about that point in the future when our love affair would be something that had happened in the past and I'd feel compelled to write about it.

■

[Orlando, Florida]
[mid-October 1957]
Dear Joyce—What you think, sweetie, I've gone and done it again. The play* is written. Please tell Leo and Joe Lustig. If Lustig wants to produce it on Broadway, I want Leo to direct, and I MUST HOWEVER BE the Advisory Director, that is, it's a true story of true real characters (Neal, Charley Mew, Al Sublette, Allen, Peter, The Bishop, Neal's wife, etc.) and I've got to show how they act. At least to Leo. I think it's good, I really dont

*Never produced in its original form.

know enuf about plays to tell if this job is a success or not, but it's done. For myself, it amuses me to read and re-read it and I can see that it would be hilarious on the stage. The stagecraft is tight, I have three Acts. First act, one scene. Second Act, two short scenes. Third act, one final long scene. Good balances. I'm sure that the first act will leave everybody bugged because it will seem short, it's funny and fast. The second act will curtain down and people will say, well maybe the Lord's on Neal's side (Zeal I'll call him) but what about this Bishop? Etc. We'll call the play BEAT GENERATION, utilizing that publicity, and also it is an accurate portrait of same. Now all I have to do is type it up, 2 copies, I'll send one to Sterling [Lord] sometime within 10 days. Tell Leo and Joe both to write me and speak out their minds what they wanta do. The main thing is the play is written. . . . it explodes in the 3rd Act, I wrote it in 24 hours because I couldn't sleep till it was finished. I feel that writing plays for me is like rolling off a log. I could do a million of them like Lope de Vega. The only trouble is my prose narratives are sadder and more beautiful, but I mustnt discount the muscles of *pure staging* of same. In other words, I'm not a judge of playcraft. Maybe someday. All I know is that the dialog is perfect because I didnt hesitate at any point in a speech, it rolls and rolls, sometimes it sounds like Shakespeare inadvertently but not often enuf of course. It's a play from real life. I could also call it that: A PLAY FROM REAL LIFE. You could if you want play a part in it, for writing money, if it got to be a hit. Nice part in it for Allen (who'd love to act) and for everybody else involved. The part of Jack is very meaty and not hard to play, like McGovern could do it. Leo would be perfect as Ginsberg (sprawling on the couch between the Bishop's mother and aunt) . . . Kelly Reynolds could easily play Neal . . . but in this part he doesnt have to be frantic at all, so anybody could play it now. . . . it isnt the Neal of On the Road but a more W.C. Fields conductor worried about horse racing and heaven. Please tell Pat MacManus also (about the Play) . . . (well I'll write to her myself) . . . I just got a big letter from Allen en route to Paris in

which he has a million instructions for me thinking I was in New
York, concerning who to call and what to do about Bill
Burroughs' manuscript [*Naked Lunch*]. I guess I'll handle all that
New Years.

Was on the road still on the bestseller list NY Times Oct.
13th or has it dropped out? Nothing down here, no papers.

If you see Lucien tell him to call Al Hendricks himself at the
Post and that I said for Al not to mention the name Lucien Carr.
To tell Al nobody wants to be busted out of jobs . . . newspaper
jobs at that. (tho that wouldnt happen but Al knows.)

I understand how tired you were that last day. . . . Yes, I ate
my 8 hamburgers and didnt even dream of a drink as usual when
I'm alone . . . but it's still too hot down here for pea soup. I have
2 orange cats, brothers, kitties, my mother and I having fun with
them. . . . I can pick up my toothbrush later but how about the
clippings? regular mail. I'm still waiting for my Grove or Pageant
money when I'll send you $20 money order. —Tell Joe Lustig def-
initely to ally himself with Ginsberg on the reading bit because
Allen knows just what and who to do. Like for instance people
like Charles Olson, Robert Creeley, of course Gregory, even
Peter, Ronnie Loewinso[h]n and others. Gary Snyder, etc. etc. In
the matter of poets, only Allen (and I) REALLY know. There are
lots of poets but only a handful of good ones. Joe must get the
best. He'd settle for Joel Chandler Harris and wouldnt even hear
of Melville.

Bob Donlin's pill was an excellent sleeper, I slept from NY to
Washington the first 4 hours like a log . . . I saw Milwaukee win
on my TV. Where's Bob now?

If Leo is traveling South tell him come see me about the
play . . . tell him to jot down 1418½ Clouser Street. If you come
with Leo where will you both stay? . . . lotsa motels . . . there's
really nothing to do here but talk. But do what you want, come
with him and we'll figure it out. Bring Joe Lustig, by God, and
we'll thrash it out (Do what you want).

Yes, go to Yaddo and dig it, see what [it]s like. Write. Get your
novel done, dont worry about whether it's good or bad, just do

it . . . it's written in the stars, you have no Power over the Stars any moren I do. The Already Stars.

I'll send that Post Clipping about John Braine to Allen so he can go to England dig the new men there.*

Yes, I've found peace in Florida and will find peace in my new pad in Long Island (Queens) this winter too, as before . . . wont have a phone or nothin, wont give address except to Lord. Thats the only way to get work done. And rest for work.

If you want to do Allen a favor call Philip Rahv at Partisan Review and ask him if he will use William Seward Burroughs' "Market" excerpt. To write Allen answer c/o American Express, Paris.

These next five years I will be so busy writing and publishing and producing I wont have time to think about l'amour . . . then, when I have a sufficient trust fund built up, I'll relax and go cruising around the world and turn my thots to love . . . and really write my greatest secret personal magic idea works for Myself . . . so dont be sad about brunettes and blondes . . . at least we are friends like 2 fingers intertwined, and I'm worried about the Joan Haverty business, doubt many things she say . . . she never sent me the divorce result. And acts funny, calling poor Lucien, of all people.

Send me all the news. Now I gotta write Don Allen, Lawrence Ferlinghetti, Allen Ginsberg, Sterling Lord and some doctor who wants me to go back to the Catholic church.

Jack

■

Joe Lustig, a new acquaintance, was one of the many opportunistically minded people who had immediately swarmed around Jack. A brash freelance press agent, somewhat down on his luck, Joe Lustig could barely afford to rent an office, much less produce a play on Broadway. In early 1958 I would make the mistake of going to work for him writing press releases, for which I was supposed to receive $50 a week off the books. Unfortunately, his checks began arriving at more

*A group of new British writers were calling themselves "the Angry Young Men."

and more irregular intervals. When I complained, Lustig stunned me by saying that he assumed I was being "kept" by Kerouac.

During his visit to New York, Jack had also taken a shine to Leo Garen, a sharp, hard-boiled, pot-smoking kid—"a 20-year-old hep-cat," Jack called him—who worked as a stage manager at the Off-Broadway production of *The Threepenny Opera*, which was a great hit that fall. Leo had asked Jack to write a play with which he could make his directorial debut. Whenever Jack met someone he liked, he would agree to give them whatever they wanted without any second thoughts. Even with reporters, whom by now he had reason to distrust, he was remarkably open, speaking to them as if they were old friends, holding nothing back. He was defenseless in his generosity.

That fall, in the waiting room at Viking Press, Jack had also met the Swiss-born photographer Robert Frank, who would become one of his closest new friends. Frank had come there in search of him, with a portfolio containing the photographs for *The Americans* under his arm. We chatted as I too waited for Jack, and I asked Robert whether I could see some of his work. "Why, that's Jack's road!" I exclaimed when I saw Frank's classic shot of a lonely road with a darkening western sky overhead. When Jack emerged from a meeting with Cowley, I introduced them and urged Jack to look at the contents of Frank's portfolio right away. Jack, as excited as I was, agreed on the spot to write an introduction for Frank's collection. The following year they would also collaborate upon the film *Pull My Daisy*, based to some extent upon the play Jack described in his letter to me.

In blasting out the play and about to start work on his new novel *Memory Babe*, Jack had evidently found "the ecstasy of mind" that had been eluding him for months. But why, I wondered, had he also swung into his wanting-to-be-a-hermit mode? By now I was getting used to his changes in mood and was trying hard not to take this one too seriously. Still, I was wounded and alarmed by Jack's warning that he had no time for love.

I discovered later that Jack was more troubled than I could possibly have imagined by the deliberately casual suggestion in my previous letter that I get a lift down to Florida to see him. Despite my growing awareness that Memere was "the villain," it would be a long time before I fully realized that Jack had to make a strict separation between the erotic side of his existence and the constraints of his life as TiJean in his mother's house. When a woman threatened to invade Memere's territory, the primal questions Jack refused to address were thrown into sharp relief.

■

Thursday, Oct. 17

Dear Jack,

WOW! . . .

Just got your letter and card in same mail. The play must be great if it boiled up in you like that. I can't wait to read it. I immediately called Leo who's awfully excited and kept talking wildly about sending you immediate telegrams. (Joe Lustig's line is busy—will add P.S. after I speak to him—I'll just tell him you wrote play and to contact Leo—my hunch is, Jack, that you're better off not getting involved with Lustig. For all his talk, he's a press agent not a *producer* (I'll bet Sterling would agree with me), and he's a bit too much of a hustler, not really sensitive—or do you think I'm just being snobbish?)—But do be careful, and remember you haven't *formally* given anything to anybody. Well, the great, happy thing is that you've written something. All your talk about not writing anything more worried me. I think you *have* to write and that you have no choice in the matter—and the biggest reason you were so bugged in NY last month was that you weren't working on anything. So you'd better keep writing until they put a tombstone over you. . . . As for l'amour, je t'aime, je t'aime—and that's really my own business, so don't try to talk me out of it, Idiot! And I will carry your toothbrush with me when I get a new apartment in January and will expect you to come in from L.I. and use it. As for Joan Haverty—I still think you should get in touch with her yourself and find out exactly what's up, so you won't have to go on feeling hunted by her (Cessa [Carr] thinks so, too!)

ROAD was on the best-seller list last Sunday (No. 15), but won't be this Sunday (according to Lucien)—I'll bet this is because the stores ran out of books—I think you'll probably be back on it again in a week or so. Oh, I'll send you all the clippings when I mail this letter, and I've sent you all the mail that's come here. Leo has made friends with Keith [Jennison] who is helping him get money for his theatre, incidentally.

I haven't seen Henri [Cru] or Bob [Donlin] again—I've been out a lot, wandering around the city and visiting old friends, haven't been able to settle down to work—so I took a 4-day job this week since I felt I might as well earn some money since I wasn't doing anything else, and now I feel like writing again and am $48 to the good. I got a letter from Yaddo and an application today too—they tell me to apply immediately so that I can get in in November, which sounds hopeful. I'll get letters from Haydn, and old Mr. Farrar. So if all goes well, I'll have a long quiet month there and maybe I'll be able to finish the novel by December. And (if you want me to) maybe I'll visit you—I mean, I would like to, but would you like me to? But maybe by that time you'll be coming North. When *are* you coming? I'm delighted that you're coming back—the city is grey and shriveled up without you. (Will you bring your cats?) I feel as though you've been gone for months. I'll make you enormous ecstasy pies . . . and I am getting thinner, although not darker . . . Does your mother feel okay about leaving Florida?

I will now try Joe Lustig, and if he's not there, I'll mail this anyhow and write you again this weekend. One moment, please. Well . . . I got Joe Lustig and *he's* all excited too, writing you immediately. Said he was going to see Sterling tomorrow anyway (before he heard about this) about drawing up a contract (????) for unwritten play. You'd better write Sterling! I told Joe you wanted Leo to direct and also told him to write Allen in Paris. (Tomorrow I'll call [Philip] Rahv about Burroughs stuff.) Leo and

Joe are going to have long talks with me tomorrow (about what, I don't know)—but I'll report back to you. Am I doing all right, Dear? So you've started a big comic confusion in NY: I can somehow picture Leo, Joe and Sterling tossing custard pies at each other. (Sterling has just gotten over Asiatic flu.) Well, laugh at this mad scene under your quiet orange tree and write another play or something.

The papers are full of war—and the city is blowing its sirens outside my window at this minute—very depressing and unreal. The only thing to do is keep on writing plays, novels, poems and stuffing these frantically into the big crack in the world until everything collapses.

Love,
Jerce

Monday

Dear Jack,

This letter from Allen came today.

Not much news: Joe Lustig had the flu and hasn't seen Sterling yet. He says he's seeing him on Friday and also says "Tell Jack I will produce his play"—whatever that means. But it all seems to be terribly legal because he's bringing his lawyer with him (he tells me that his lawyer represents Paramount as well as independent companies—and that they're going to talk to Sterling about a movie of ON THE ROAD.) Also, Leo and Joe haven't spoken to each other yet, and somehow I feel that they don't really want to. (Have you heard from either of them?) Joe is giving me a book of Hemingway's poems to send to you (????).

I called Partisan Review today and found out that Burroughs's ms. is still being read (which they said was a good sign), and Allen's poem is going to be in the Winter issue.* I'll write Allen

*Despite this show of interest, *Partisan Review* was actually very hostile to the Beat writers, fearing a shift of power. When Hettie Jones stopped working there in 1959 to have a baby, I took over her job for six months.

and tell him this. Joe has sent Allen a postcard which he says reads: "Jack Kerouac told me to get in touch with you. I can make you a star." What on earth will Allen make of that!

The Post interview wasn't in the paper this weekend either—instead there was a long thing on the new secretary of defense. Maybe next week. Maybe Pat MacManus knows—she's asked me to have lunch with her tomorrow, so I'll find out then.

What you doing? Have you started the new book yet? And did you get a typewriter finally?

I'm writing sporadically. You're quite right about finishing the novel—but I'm having trouble with it. It's changing, or I'm changing—anyway the rhythm of it seems different somehow. And I'm starting to be worried about money—I hope I'll know about Yaddo soon, one way or the other. But—I've found an apartment that I can have in January when I have to give up this place, and that's awfully good luck. It's in the Village and not too expensive—with a decent-sized kitchen for a change. What else? I've had my hair cut. Donald Cook got married suddenly yesterday. Ed Stringham and I got drunk together in the West End, and I saw La Traviata with parents who wept, but I didn't. So you can see life is quiet in these parts. I feel dull and wear long black stockings and am reading THE POSSESSED which gets greater and greater. On Saturday, I was walking along Fifth Avenue, thinking about you and suddenly saw your face on the back of a copy of THE TOWN AND THE CITY that a girl was carrying—strange, strange.

Love from your foreign correspondent,
Jerce

I hear that John Holmes has sold another article on the Beat Generation.

[Orlando, Florida]
[mid-October 1957]

Dear Joyce

Here is your money order for 20. I wanted to write a long letter but this is just a note to go with the money order, I have to shave now and got to post office and bank first . . . I'm typing last act of play today and will insert things in it Peter O. says because it's way too short!—you said 120 pages, and it'll only be 90 as is . . . however, the play is there, the nucleus, the meat, the form, the "baby meat"— I'll write you a long letter in a coupla days. . . . Received long scroll-letter from Leo, great, I told him about Lillian Hellman* etc. and that LH might not take it anyhow. . . . I also wrote to Lucien & Cess— I hope you're right about bestseller list return. . . . Hope you get to Yaddo, or else why dont you just leave phone off hook and finish your novel, tell everybody you went to Yaddo!

I'll write this week.

Jack

[Orlando, Florida]
[mid-October]

Dear Joyce

Thanks for your letters which help me a great deal, make me happy, a little lonely down here . . . & they always have such interesting news. Rye & coke at my desk here, near at hand, dont drink beer anymore, it's the Lucien Drink from now on and because my mother makes great supper every night at 8 I haven't been drunk once, just high, since I got back . . . Very happy life now. Especially with the great news, of Road back on bestseller list for next Sunday, NUMBER ELEVEN!, and Sterling tells me it's because the Book Find club took it and a telegram from Lucien CHIN UP BOY BESTSELLER AGAIN NEXT SUNDAY NUMBER ELEVEN JERCE PROBABLY CORRECT ABOUT SCARCITY LUCIEN

*Hellman had expressed interest in seeing the play for a possible Broadway production.

(Just got it 10 minutes ago) I'd written to Lucien and told him what you said, also to find Joan Haverty number, also a joke we forgot to tell Blair.

What Joe Lustig is doing, bringing his lawyer and Paramount and all that sounds alright, but I want Brando to take it. . . . Sterling says Brando interested, tho on honeymoon. Dean Moriarty gotta be INTELLIGENT, not just hotrodder. I wrote to Allen, explain'd Lustig to him, "star" etc. Say, Pat MacManus must be flipping out over Road development, hey? I TOLD THEM SO, remember, in bar, world series, it will be Number One by Christmas I said. Could be. How many copies Book Find Club? I studied my contract and see that I would get 20 cents for every copy either way, outright sale or royalties on 60 percent discount. Financial genius.

What I doing? Just finished typing play today, perfect play now, pulled things out of VISIONS OF NEAL and DESOLATION ANGELS and stuck em in, it wasnt long enuf, by 40, well 25 pages. Now it's a 103-page ms. But with only double spaces between dialog, therefore quite long and dialog will have to be spoke FAST. Next job, the novel for Viking, about childhood, will rent typewriter for a month, as mine own may be coming back before Xmas, from Germany, where it was mistakenly routed.

Hope $20 help your money problem. Ask Giroux help you Yaddo. He got me to go there once and I didn't go. Great apartment, in the Village! Donald Cook crazy, why marry? what's wrong with just lovin? Strange about Fifth Ave., Town & City girl, etc. Where is John Holmes' article on Beat at? what mag?

Wrote Leo, long letter, Leo great, love Leo, somewhere along the line Leo and I make it financially and artistically you watch. My play too *mad* maybe for 45th St., Leo take it. My play fine now: first act craziest thing on stage since Aristophanes squat. Real life not Saroyanesquelike.

Joyce, fore I forget, pick up that I.E. copy of yours and give me address of editorial office in Cambridge, them bastards stole

Lucien Midnight 40-page prose piece, Fletcher's the cad, the villain. Mike McClure wants it now, to publish in his new Hazelwood Press. I heard the Evergreen Recording of Poets, very great, Allen Great, Rexroth great, Ferlinghetti too, McClure too, Josephine Miles too. Did Lustig hear it? Ferlinghetti coming to visit me in Florida. Is Leo coming next month or not? He's coming with a guy and another girl, why dont you just settle down in Yaddo and finish FLY NOW PAY LATER. I'll see you in January anyway. Nothing down here but scorpions, lizards, vast spiders, mosquitos, vast cockroaches & thorns in the grass—hot—awful—ugh—I go back L.I. Love

Jack

x

A tangerine fell directly on the middle of my head today as I was trying to decide whether to call God "it" or "Him" — Whattayou think? Right on my middle sconce, right on the middle pate, right out of a tree.

Allen urgent letter concerned going to Northport saving Lafcadio from shrewish mother wants to commit him to madhouse or cops—Allen thot I was in NY still—Would Stringham go save him? Allen will write—Peter so worried he about to come back at once, next week.

LATEST PERM

October is the sweetest month.
Apples are sweeter,
   leaves are sweeter,
      (TASTE EM IN THE SPRING AND SEE)
I am sweeter because sadder
October is the sweetest month.
My bed is sweeter.
My art, my dart,
   my lingering part
      (AS I DEPART FROM ACT THREE)
It makes me madder & madder.

A POEM FOR EMILY*
Sweet Emily Dickinson
who played with your hair?
who counted the pimples
on your moonlight chin?
who wiped away the smut
of your disregard of natural
phenomena in hairy men?
who taught you love of cock?
who taught you cunt?
O sweet Emily, if death
Stopped on your proud door,
did I, the lily weep?
did I, the marble sarco
phagus, bleed iron chocolate
tears? Meet you in the
c h u r c h y a r d

                                                    Monday
Dear Jack,
    Hooray for Number 11! And just to make it real—here's the
clipping. Ha! I told you so!
    New York's buzzing again. Wish you were here. I've been
talked into giving a vast chaotic party Saturday night. Why don't
you come? Lucien and Cessa are coming, Pat, Leo, the Franks,
various Columbia people, etc. and 85 people I've never met probably—in this apartment! Imagine the confusion! If you don't
show up, I'll write you a blow-by-blow description. Then I will
clean up the debris and go, I hope, to Yaddo—haven't heard yet,
but they've written to all my references and I dreamt that they
sent my ms. all over the world and got reports back from Japan,
England, etc.—they congratulated me on weird things like "the
brilliant use of the new vocabulary, in particular the word 'subor-

*Jack also enclosed a sketch of "Stanley Gould with hat."

dinate,'" but they decided not to accept me because my ms. was messy and full of little blue lines which they found quite disturbing, and which somehow proved that I was a member of the Underground!—perhaps a prophetic dream. Pat, by the way, tells me that Keith Jennison will be up there [at Yaddo] in November. Also other messages from Pat: 1) John Holmes article will be in Esquire in Nov. and will be mainly about you; at the same time, Harper's Bazaar, Pageant and Playboy will appear—and she thinks this will help push the book up a little higher. 2) she's going to find out what happened to the Post article this week. 3) Tom Prideaux* would very much like to read your play—he knows lots of producers and things.

Jack, have you or are you going to write to Edward about Lafcadio? I haven't been able to get in touch with him. Not sure it will work out. Ed's kind of drunk and suicidal lately—on the other hand, he might like taking care of someone. The thing is that Lafcadio is a pretty hung-up kid and it won't do much good to bring him from one vacuum into another. Anyway—Howard [Schulman] is going to drive out to Northport on Wednesday and see if he can bring Laf back with him (this is good because he knows Laf better than anyone else here in NY now.) If things fall through with Edward, Laf can probably stay with Howard for a while since Howard has a big apartment. But just when is Peter coming back?—this is important. Another problem is money— we don't know whether Laf is in good enough shape to work and both Howard and I are broke and can't afford to see him through and we don't know whether Ed would be willing to either (although *he* could do it—but Ed doesn't like to be "inconvenienced," if you know what I mean). Could you send some money for Lafcadio if necessary? *But do find out about Peter!* Well, I suppose I might as well write to Allen and Peter tonight and tell them about all this, altho' nothing's happened yet. Howard, by the way, would take very good care of Lafcadio,—he's a gentle

*Pat's friend, who reported on entertainment and culture for *Time* magazine.

person really—I think all that business about stealing was just an act.

About I.E.—it's no longer in business, the offices have been closed for six months. But one of the editors, Leo Raditsa, works for Readers Subscription in N.Y. He'd probably know where your ms. was. Why don't you write him. Or, if you'd like,—I'll call, if that's any help.

Saw the Franks yesterday. They're great! And they have two wild, beautiful children, who rode screaming and yelling on the backs of Howard and Leo—who collapsed exhausted. You must visit the Franks when you come back. Robert wants very much to make a movie with you. Maybe you could write a script that Peter O. [Orlovsky] could be in.

What else? I've written a new chapter. Leo is in love with a young, beautiful rock-and-roll singer and is in hotter and hotter pursuit of the dollar—it disturbs me to hear him talk so much about money—I'm sure he'll be great someday, but right now he should be just a young kid having a ball without having to worry about Wall Street and fat movie producers. Howard also is in love with a plain, sensible Barnard girl—and called me up at 4:00 A.M. to announce that fact: "Joyce! It's Howard! I'm in love! I'm in love! I'm in love! Oh . . . were you really sleeping?"

What's with the play, the novel, movies, you, cats? Have you been hit by any more tangerines—did you make God "he" at that point?—but perhaps tangerines just have a will of their own. I *like* your mad perms. But don't be sadder and madder. Goodnight. I kiss you in Florida and must run now to put this in the mail. By the middle of the week everything will have erupted and I'll write you from Pompeii.

Love,
Jerce

P.S. The $20 was beautiful and vanished instantly.
P.S. Don't worry about length of play. If you're typing it with characters' names on left side of page followed by colon and speeches are single-spaced, you probably have more than enough.

And anyway length problems are always worked out in production.

P.S. Do any Frisco people write you and mention Elise? I hear she's broke and in trouble, arrested for drunkenness. I'm worried. Never got another letter from her.

■

Howard Schulman had been a good friend of Elise's and mine since our Barnard days. Burning with energy, good-hearted, and chronically schizophrenic, he wrote poems heavily influenced by Kerouac and Ginsberg; his daredevil driving was in the tradition of Neal Cassady. Since Howard was the only person I knew who had a car, I'd enlisted him to drive me out to Northport for my visits to Lafcadio, Peter Orlovsky's brother.

My fleeting impressions of Northport, which reminded me of a New England fishing village, with its harbor and white Cape houses, would prove fateful for Jack. When he began to seriously think about moving his mother up north and settling in Long Island, I told him I thought Northport—only forty miles from Manhattan—might be the right place for him.

■

[Orlando, Florida]
Nov. 1, 1957

Dear Joycey

Dig my new typewriter! A Royal standard, I'm renting it for $7.73 a month (ugh) but if I do buy it they will deduct that from the $89.50 price . . . and I think I will buy it cause it's a bitch, with a good firm fast touch, nice small keys, nice quiet sound, direct keys (unlike my lost typewriter that had indirect jointed keys for the silencer equipment and they tended to jam) . . . on this machine I can swing and swing and swing and swing. I think I can go 95 words a minute on this one after a week of practice, as now. . . . The movers owe me a chick a check for $100 for the lost one . . . so I'll buy it . . . and this is such a good typewriter that all I do is yak and yak about nothing interesting.

Now I'll type up all my poems and prose, which has been lying around in my boxes in hand script—

I'll be curious to see what happens to On the Road this week. Lemme know, I dont get the Times here. That Saturday night party must be (must have been) wild . . . quite a combination of people. I'm glad to hear about Howard's alright, yes I did think he was kidding about stealing, he hasnt got mean eyes like the poet who did steal. He has luminous good eyes. . . . So tell me about Laf and if Howard got him: and by the way: Allen says to send money for Lafcadio, if and when needed, and deduct it off the $225 I owe him. I'm expecting news of Peter any day and their plans for what to do. . . .

I'll look for that John Holmes article: I'm surprised and gratified about his writing about me. . . . Post article: I've written to Hendrix [sic] myself, reassuring him to go ahead.

Tom Prideaux: I have the carbon copy of the play here, soon's I hear from Sterling who's been silent because of illness, I'll send it into his office for anybody wants to read it other than Lillian Hellman. Leo or Tom Prideaux, or both.

I also bought a roll of white teletype paper that reaches from Orlando Fla. to NYCity . . . huge, a dollar forty, I'm all set to go now: also I will type up my final translation of the Vajracheddikaprajnaparamita on a long 12 foot roll and read it like a torah scroll every morning.

Dont worry about your dream, dreams are not prophetic at all, put no stock in dreams & omens. (They DO prophesy, but on a subconscious level that has nothing to do with conscious life.)

Please give me Leo Raditsa's full address: and better, call him and ask him directly [about] the Lucien Midnight manuscript, about 24 pages of prose . . . Mike McClure wants it at once.

Also, Sterling Lord is looking for Robt. Frank about the introduction for Grove as well as for France . . . so please tell Robt. to call Sterling, or give Sterling Robt's phone number. My little secretary.

Yes I certainly can write a movie about Peter, for Robt Frank to photograph . . . we'll see about movies. . . . Sterling is quiet on the subject, only says that the interest in Hollywood hasn't reached a head yet, that Brando is on a honeymoon, etc. Sterling hasnt commented on the play yet, or said he received it, I think he's sick in bed or something. Call him & see. My little secretary. With the long black stockings. The cats are fine, two of them, we'll keep them both and bring them to NY in the Spring. I wanta live out in Elmhurst on the Sound (that place where Jerry Newman's father has an estate and Jerry* has a cottage) instead of Richmond Hill, if I sell book to movies that is, and establish trust fund. Otherwise we'll have to start in Queens. The novel for Malcolm [Cowley] I'll start that now, montha November good month for writing. Childhood. The title: MEMORY BABE (my boyhood nickname cause I remembered everything) . . . No word from Elise, why dont you write to Elise care of The Place bar and grille, Grant St., SF . . . (dont have number) . . . Or care of City Lights Bookshop, 261 Columbus Ave, San Francisco 11, Calif.—

Eating tangerines now, but I saved the one that fell on my head, if you come here with Leo you can eat it, it'll be delicious in a month. No, it was just such a personal slap on the head at that moment, I was surprised, nay awakened into something: just as silly to call God a Personal God as an Impersonal. What the hell.

The return of the black cowboy.
The black cowboy hides
    under the automobile,
    pulls out his serpent,
and eats.
	THE SEA IS MY BROTHER
	   —Big whitemouth
	     osh, Neptune, sceptred,
	  a leg in the gray
	     air uncaring, an arm
	  on mossy underwaters,
	  nose away,

*An old prep school friend, now a record producer.

          contempt, he waited
          beyond the two lighthouse
          towers—flat as death.

I just got Allen Ginsberg's Guggenheim form, I have to recommend him, which I'll do mightily. It's funny (this is confidential)
what he says to them: i.e.
   a. Significance of its presumable contribution to arts:
Unpredictable
   b. Present state of project: Already begun
   c. Expectation as to completion: In Time.
   d. Places: Europe, Orient, & America
   e. Authorities: None
   f. Expectation of publication: Promised to City Lights
   g. Ulimate purpose as artist: To write an ecstatic poem of spir-
itual reality.

                    So there!
      He also says: "Worked alone, consulted W.C.
      Williams and Jack Kerouac on poetry, 1948–1956"
             what, I mean wha, I mean, wha?
It pleases me, he never told me I was a poet to my face (hoping I
wouldnt get spoiled, I see now)

          PERM—ESKIMOS IN GREENLAND
             were hanging out the wash
             against the iron orange blood
             of stony loveless skies
             with wires of animal thong
             in a bleaker igligloogloo backyard
             than I'd ever known
             in poor Pawtucketville

             GREGORY'S LATESTPERM
          "When once as a boy I came upon
             in a room of poverty

                    ____
                     93

the sad pursued runaways of sky
I called to my dreamfather
And wept elemental things
From the mercy of his eyes"
                    Gregory adds in a note:
        "I am weak and awesomely incidental."
                        (!)
Well, Joyce, enuf of this,
write as often as you want,
I'll answer every letter double
                    As ever,
                        love,
                            Jack
LATEST NEWS: Just got telegram from Sterling: CAN YOU
HAVE PLAY RETYPED SO THAT I HAVE 3 MORE COPIES
BRANDO INTERESTED   LETTER FOLLOWS   REGARDS
STERLING

And from Leo SEND LORD SCRIPT AND LETTER POST
HASTE LETTER FOLLOWING LOVE LEO (Apparently
Brando had read On the Road, I hope he wont be disappointed by
the play which is only a "light comedy" in a sense, perhaps not.)
                        (Tell Leo I will do)

                            [early November 1957]
                            Bad Monday,

Dear Jack,
    I dig your typewriter: Beautiful!
    Ugh! What a week. I wouldn't give you two cents for it.
Everything fell through. Didn't get out to see Lafcadio after all
because Howard had exams and couldn't make it and he's the
only one who has a car (which is necessary because no one has
Laf's exact address, but Howard remembers where the house is
approximately). So when you write to Allen, tell him it'll be next

Saturday for sure, and then I'll write and tell him what happened in detail. That's fine about the money.

I am typing this letter mainly with my left hand since I've developed a strange disease of the right elbow, known as bursitis. I think I'm too young to get it but anyway I have it, and it's a big drag. Very painful last week, couldn't use my right arm, had to quit job and sit at home with hot compresses. I couldn't even write!—I guess the one a thing a writer definitely needs is his right arm. It's getting better though now. I cleaned the house with my left hand and gave the party—it was a DISASTER. Someone in the West End heard about it and arrived with fifteen nowhere people. And lots of people I wanted to come couldn't make it because of Asian flu, lack of baby-sitters, etc. It was that kind of party. Henri came, lovely Henri with the biggest bottle of whiskey I've ever seen. Also Pat MacManus, who circulated madly and kept telling me it was a *wonderful* party and asking Who's that person over there? How did *he* get here? She came with Bill Cole* who leered at all the girls Jesuitically. And somehow—don't ask me how—Gabriel Katz appeared. I got drunker than I've ever been, couldn't stand up, passed out and awoke Sunday morning in the middle of hundreds of cigaret butts, and all the lights on, millions of bottles, potato chips, lost umbrellas, scarves, corkscrews, and one persimmon lying mysteriously on the living-room floor. The doorbell rang. I tottered to the door, discovering that I had an awful hangover, and there was a special delivery letter from Yaddo announcing very politely that I had *not* gotten in because their schedule was all filled, etc. etc. (How's that for omens?) So now I guess I'll have to get a steady job eventually, like pretty soon. Meanwhile, I have this temporary thing and will just write every night and all weekend, won't see anyone. But I did want to get out of the city, damn it!

*The director of publicity at Knopf.

Heard news of Elise—that she'd been arrested for drunkenness. What a sinister, horrible thing to happen to her—like the reality of all her worst dreams! I'm very worried about her. If I had lots of money, I'd fly out and see her. She hasn't written me yet.

I don't know . . . sometimes I feel like volunteering to go to the moon . . . or just going—anywhere. I'm beginning to appreciate Leo's nervousness about money. Money is freedom, but nothing more, nothing more—being wealthy isn't the point of it at all. I don't really want to go to the moon—I want to see you. Talking to most people is like spitting into the air. Days, weeks go by and nothing *said*. Maybe in a few weeks I'll pick up and come see you . . . can I? . . . I don't think Leo will make it somehow . . . but some people I know are driving as far as Georgia, and I've got some money from this temporary job. Would you like me to come down for a little while? I'd be very quiet and bring pads and pads of yellow paper with me. . . .

Hey, you're still on the bestseller list—Number 14. And your picture's in Harper's Bazaar, lovely, looks just like you, except that one of your ears is missing, but anyway you're a handsome bastard, and Martha Bacon wrote about you quite intelligently, talked about "beat" being "beatific" and compared ON THE ROAD to HUCK FINN. . . .

That's great about Brando! And I think he would be interested in a comedy—he has a marvellous comic sense—witness, Stanley Kowalski (did you see him in the movie of STREET-CAR?) And don't say "only a light comedy"—they're just about the hardest things to write. And you are a poet, always a poet—ON THE ROAD's a poem as much as THE SEA IS MY BROTHER (that's beautiful!). I wrote a poem about Elise this week—maybe I'll send it, maybe I won't—will decide when I type envelope.

> love,
> from your left-handed, black-
> stockinged, hung-up amie,
> Jerce

[enclosure]

THE DEPARTURE OF ELISE FROM THE CITY
Elise
got on the Greyhound Bus.

Having sabotaged
a few of the clocks
in the city—
she left me the rest,
and a destiny
of endless chop-suey,
a beat-up copy of *The Idiot*.
She didn't own much.

When the electrical doors closed
and the air-conditioning began,
the black leather roads
took her.

Her friends
celebrate her departure
with beer and a fist fight.
Her parents
In their impenetrable living-room
Have drawn the blinds.

[Orlando, Florida]
Nov 12

Dear Joyce

I was waiting to hear from you, but now I'll write anyway,
expecting any day news of Laf and all . . . and it's my strong
hunch that Allen & Peter are both on their way back on a ship
right this minute, because I havent head from them in 2 weeks or
more.

Joyce, dont come down to Florida, I've started on my novel
and I want to work on it every day and night until it's time to go

to New York, probably before Xmas, and besides there's no room for you, you'd have to sleep on an Army cot next to my mother's couch in the kitchen-livingroom-bedroom and the only other room is my small room which, when you want to go to toilet, you have to close the door (of) and besides there's nothing we can do here in the way of going out (no car) or any kinda fun. Okay? I'll be seeing you shortly anyway. It would be a waste of train fare, $80 roundtrip to be exact. I havent sold any movies or plays to anybody lately and until then I wont squander my food money from the short stories.

Enclosed is a letter I want you to mail to Hiram Haydn with no return address on the envelope. Just type out the Random address, which I have no way of knowing down here. In it I try to recommend Holmes* to Haydn, and why . . . (mention you). (Tho you don't need it.)

I'm mad today at Ferlinghetti who asked to see my poems and then said there were too many of them to publish, as if he couldnt make a selection. Just to nose around my unpublished manuscripts. I hate poets because they dont love poetry, they hate it. If there's anything they hate it's somebody else's poems. I can just see them bristling like porcupines. Thank God for the Zen Lunatic Gary [Snyder], Allen, Gregory, [Philip] Whalen & Burroughs.

By the way, your Elise poem very beautiful, Black leather road. Hm. And incidentally, I asked Mike McClure of Frisco to call up the Place and find out about Elise and he says nobody remembers her there. There's just nobody I know that knows her. I know, I'll send a big false report to my agents in Frisco announcing that Allen has actually returned to NY and Elise'll hear it and come back home. Okay?

Thanks for calling Raditsa. If he *did* give it to Allen dont tell me he went and lost that too. . . . he's already lost the precious manuscripts of Neal Cassady, two of them. Like accident-prone.

*John Clellon Holmes was trying to sell his second novel, *The Horn*, to Random House.

Glad to hear your novel a good clip last week and you happy again. . . . Yesterday, in 4 hours, I typed up the 12,000 word Diamond Sutra on a long 12-foot scroll, beautiful, with my final transliteration, one of the most precious religious documents in the world, even you'll like it when you read it. —Tonight, on a 20 foot roll, whang whang on MEMORY BABE. And then sleep late tomorrow. And every day till Dec. 1st, then type it. I have a lot of work to do, and so do you, we'll go a-larking when we're done.

Write soon . . . .
Jean Louis*

Tuesday, Nov. 12

Dear Jack,

Dig the enclosed [best-seller] list—if you haven't already!

On Saturday, Howard and I finally got out to see Lafcadio on trip from which we almost didn't return alive—I'll describe gory details later. Unfortunately, Laf was alone and we didn't get to see his mother (by the way, was it Laf who wrote to Peter or Mrs. O.?). We told Laf we'd get him a room and see that he'd have lots of company, etc., but the upshot of the whole thing is that he wants to stay where he is, doesn't like the city—but I think this is perhaps because we must have scared him coming in upon him suddenly out of the night when he hadn't seen anyone in months (you have no idea how quiet it is out there), with Howard being hysterically friendly and shouting: "Come on Laf, pack up, we're going to take you to the city, Man! We'll get you a room in a big hotel, a job, and a broad. Wouldn't you like a broad? Come *on*, Laf!" And picture Lafcadio in this tiny room no bigger than my bathroom, mainly taken up by an old stove, with pictures on the wall from the Frick Museum which I think Elise had given him, reading Rimbaud and a book called "From Baudelaire to the Surrealists" and drawing pictures in crayon and delicate pencil

*Jack's French Canadian name.

lines on the end papers of the books because he had no other paper (one was a picture of a boy lying face down on the shore of an immense sea)—and there we were screaming about New York and broads. He kept saying "What? What did you say?" and asking where's Allen, where's Jack, where's Peter, over and over again—he seemed so vague and way out. When we asked him how he was getting along with his mother, he said, "She's having trouble with her teeth." So, Jack, I don't know . . . He's going to come to NY this week to see his father and says he'll call us, but I don't know whether he will. Maybe if we're with him and things are calmer, he'll begin to want to come to the city—I'm not even sure he should, frankly (Perhaps not unless he's with Peter or someone he knows very well). But it's awful to see anyone so isolated, especially someone 17 years old. At any rate, Howard and I are going to try to see him once a week—we'll take him around the city, make him feel more in touch with things—I wish we knew some young kids he could get to know. And this way, we'll at least be right on the spot if anything happens with his mother. What do you think? And could you convey all this to Allen and Peter? I gave Laf your address, and I'd give you his except that Howard's the one who wrote it down and I can't get in touch with him, but I think you should write him, he talked about you a lot. If you send the letter in care of me, I'll know the address by the time it arrives.

The ride with Howard scared the hell out of me. He was doing 80–90, whizzing in and out of lanes. When we got out to Northport, we didn't know Laf's address and went up the wrong perpendicular dirt road with no room to turn around and come down, so I walked 5 feet ahead of the car shouting Right! Left! while Howard drove with the door open, but he couldn't hear me after all. Then—on the way back, Howard was doing 80 again and we smacked into a car making a U-turn and almost landed upside down in a ditch, but it's the other guy's fault because he didn't have his lights on, so Howard's going to collect $1000 and buy a new car (he's in ecstasy, says he's been praying for an accident). The car still worked so we drove in it back to the city—by this time Howard was getting a little nervous and he kept cutting a car in front of us off the road—it turned out there were two policemen in it, so we got a ticket (by this time we were laughing hysterically). The policemen said to H.: "Your car's a little banged up," and H. said, "Oh yes, we're just coming from an accident." I'm afraid if we drive out to Northport every weekend, we'll be dead in a month.

I'm coming out of last week's gloom (I must have written you a scary letter. Sorry). It was just that there seemed to be no end to things that were going to fall through, but this week I don't care! Also, I really do like to "kvetch" sometimes (isn't that a marvellous Yiddish word! It means just what it sounds like). My arm healed finally and I'm able to work again. But everybody up here is blue, tired, sad—maybe just because it's November, which has always seemed to me a soggy Germanic sentimental month. Leo's bitter and frustrated, just about hugged out of his mind— he's smoking tea a lot. If you were here, we could all be gloomy together and sit on Second Avenue moaning into our beer and accumulating disasters. Think what you're missing! By January, everybody will be resigned to everything, and you will arrive full of hope, jumping with your cats. I saw the Franks again—they are depressed like everyone else but very happy about the new intro, which I read—it's terrific! a real ecstatic poem (glad you kept the line about the coffin). Leo dangled your play in front of me for fifteen minutes, but that's all, and I didn't get to read it, damn it! What's with Marlon Brando?—I hear he's in NY now. Did you hear from Raditsa yet? How's MEMORY BABE? Write!

Love,
Jerce
xxxx

Friday, 11/15/57

Dear Jack,

Got your letter and I guess you have mine by now. I mailed your note to [Hiram] Haydn (I hear from my spies at MCA that

Random accepted THE HORN this week, incidentally—and that Haydn's very enthusiastic about it!).

This is a short letter sneaked in at the office and is mainly to tell you to write to me at my parents' address for the next two weeks (620 West 116th Street, NY 27). I found a marvellous apartment on 13th Street near Second Avenue and will be moving there in 2 weeks—meanwhile, someone has taken over my sublet. (The apartment in the Village I told you about fell through the week that everything else did.) This new place is quite comfortable—and *very cheap*, so if I don't get a regular job until I finish the book, I'll be able to manage anyway. We can dig the East Side when you come back! Hundreds of stores with olives and pomegranates and enormous cheeses!

You're right, I know, that I shouldn't come down now and that I should settle down to work. Everyone is being rather stern with me, in fact. I've been looking for a regular job—not too enthusiastically—but somehow I find it's easier for me to work on the book when I feel that I haven't got much time to myself. Unfortunately, I find myself saying things on interviews that don't exactly inspire confidence, such as—

Question: Miss G., do you intend to have a career in publishing?
Answer: Oh, publishing's all right, I guess, if you *have* to work. (which is really the way I feel about all that now.)

Just as I thought—Lafcadio never called. I'll try to go out and see him this weekend. Any news from Allen yet? Do you really think he's en route?

Next time I hear from you, I bet you'll say you've just finished MEMORY BABE—I'm very jealous, it isn't fair, etc. etc.

> Love
> from your lazy secretary (red-
> stockinged this week),
> Joyce

Dear Jack,

Hey! Long Silence! what's been happening? How's MEMORY
BABE etc.?

I've had a very complicated week. Got a job finally at Dover
Press, a paperback house. Not very exciting, but I'm awfully
relieved. It looked for a while like there weren't any jobs.
Publishers are closing up, laying off people (the same "depression"
that's fouling things up for Leo's theatre). So I'm working for Mr.
Hayward Cirker, who is a very dull man and one of the least
charming people I've ever met. He asks questions like: Are you
intelligent? What is your I.Q.? Do you consider yourself assidu-
ous? Do you derive pleasure from the typing of letters, memos and
contracts? (How could anyone in their right mind get pleasure
from *that*? I keep smiling vaguely and don't say much, tear out at
five o'clock.) Cirker is definitely one of Allen's Mustard Gas editors. I've managed to sneak a lot of time for my novel, though—
and I've got an electric typewriter to write on! Sweetie, you don't
know what a typewriter is until you've tried an electric one—
incredibly fast. Get very, very rich and buy yourself one. Better
than a swimming pool. Henri tells me you're getting a tape
recorder and you're going to sit him down with it when you're up
here. I saw Henri last night—Pat MacManus gave a cocktail
party. Henri arrived with someone he calls "the funniest man in
the world" and a gallon of Canadian Club in an enormous bottle.
Pat flipped, couldn't believe Henri wanted to give it to her, kept
saying "Now we'll just look at it because it's so beautiful and then
you take it home. . . ." (this said very earnestly and school-
teacherishly). But Henri said at last: "*I* am a Frenchman and *I* am
giving you this bottle." (But he said it much better than that.)
Henri had a long conversation with Fran Evans* about horse racing—Did you know that she plays the horses? She even knows
details about horse-studding (?) which she discusses in her sweet
little Ivy League voice, but alas, she doesn't like Frenchmen.

*She was Pat MacManus's assistant.

Henri's going to move me on Sunday into my new apartment on 13th Street—the third time he's moved me in six months!

Listen, Tom Prideaux, who was at the party, said he saw Brando at lunch and asked him about ON THE ROAD. Brando hadn't read it yet himself but was quite interested, altho' he said he was worried that there wasn't a solid enough story. Too bad you can't meet him and talk to him yourself. He'll be in NY for a while, I think. There was a long article about him by Truman Capote in the New Yorker (did you see it?)—a very nasty article, most of it lies probably, but I think it would interest you any-way—it talks about Brando being interested in Zen, etc. I'll try to dig it up for you, if you like?

I've been living with my parents for almost two weeks now in my old room, which is still painted pink and has empty book-shelves. It was a mistake to move back, even for a little while—it got them all upset. My mother keeps asking, But why can't you stay with us! And whenever any of my friends call up, she says, Don't tell Joyce, but I'm very concerned about her, and tries to get information about me secretly. It's like living in the middle of a spy ring. And my father's gotten so old suddenly, feels tired all the time. I took a walk with him one day and a newsboy called him "pops"—I almost felt like crying. (We were looking for my father's bookie but when we came to his usual corner, he wasn't there, but five cops were—then we saw him ducking into Barnard of all places.)

Haven't been able to get out to see Laf again. Howard's car, for some strange reason, isn't functioning.

When are you coming up, do you think? You wrote me some-thing about "before Christmas"; Henri says late January. Hope it's soon. I miss you.

My permanent address from Thursday on will be: 338 East 13th Street—even though I won't have all my stuff in till Sunday.

Write soon!

Love,
Joyce

P.S. I'm reading Suzuki's writings on Zen Buddhism.

[Orlando, Florida]
[December 17, 1957]
H W Mustapha Nightsoil King of the Tits
1937 in the age of the Beat New Yorker
Dec 1786th, 1964524385

Hack'

Ho'

Lissen Joyce, longsilence because writing new novel which
is not memory babe at all, but THE DHARMA BUMS, greater
than On the Road and however only half finished & right in
midst of my starrynight exstacies contemplating how to wail &
finish it I get big phone call poopoo from Sterling Lord says
Millstein arranging for me to read my work over mike in Village
Vanguard nightclub for salary per week so will do for money and
for excuse to come back New York. Will live at Henri's around
the corner & sleep all day, also type my new novel on his
machine at dusk, then Henri and I dress up and sally forth to my
2 daily performances in the Vanguard. If this doesnt kill me nothing will. Imagine all my friends in the audience. I'll just be a cool
sound musician and act cool, that's what. But the money is grand
and I'll take it: I wanta buy me a stationwagon and disappear
with my rucksack into the West this spring, thats what. Leo has
tinhorn ideas about the art of the play, his letter betrays that, my
play is admittedly too short but outsida that it's something new &
fresh, a SITUATIONLESS PLAY FOR FUTURE PEOPLE. Leo'll
end up producing tinhorn plays for TV, you watch. For money.
I'm not money mad, that's why I'm an artist. I wont write back to
Leo. As for Marlon Brando, he can go fuck himself. I dont care
about these tinhorn show people. What do I care? If I had to go
and apply for jobs like you do, they'd have to drag me into
Bellevue in two days. I couldnt stand it. That's why I am and will
be always a bum, a dharma bum, a rucksack wanderer. Why didnt
Henri show up with his girl, Dell Marshall? He must be brooding
now. As for Fran, she oughta appreciate Henri if she had any
sense . . . she ain't so ivy league, to me, as like a Catholic nothing. I mean all that whining business of not spreading her legs in

the name of the Devil, and in God she dont believe. Cancerous. To say the least, my dear. In fact, she is my 2nd wife to a T. My 2nd wife just had twins with her new Arab husband. That's good. And they'll adopt the girl child which is sposed to be mine. Truman Capote . . . what'd he say about Brando? I spose poor Marlon wouldnt let Truman blow him a few years ago. No Leo Raditsa hasn't sent me Lucien Midnight and I dont blame it on him but on Corso who begged me for the ms. promising he would rather die than lose it so he lost it and lives. I'll write to Laf, the only pure one in the bunch, with the exception of Burroughs and Cassady. Allen and Greg sent me their latest poems from Paris. Greg says "There are old sweetlys in sun-arc! gentle grand-ninnies" . . . and Allen says "O my poor mother with eyes of Ma Rainey dying in an ambulance" . . . new pomes. If your Pop is old what makes you think birth doesnt equal death and that you wont grow old yourself and be a little ole rainpot of flowers on a dusty window in Lower Manhattan in 1969. I told ya, I told ya. Why dont you just get drunk with Lucien and Cessa. I'm coming to New York for the gentle sweetlys of sun-arc in December and I'll see you. I'm going to live with Henri because I want to sleep while he works all day and I want to be in the Village and I want to watch his TV and I want to talk with him for a month and I dont want to importune you any further because as I told you I'm an Armenian and I dont wanta get married till I'm 69 and have 69 gentle grandninnies. Please dont be mad at me, I wanta be alone, Greta Garbo. This is going to be the greatest fiasco in his-tory of American Literature, this Village Vanguard shot.* I'm going to write the funniest comedy in the history of American Theater, I'm going to keep a daily diary of everything that's going to happen, including Henri's dialogs. p.s. You'll know all about what Suzuki talks about after you've read if ever Dharma Bums.

Jack.

*On November 30, Jack wrote Allen Ginsberg, "I am afraid of this coming New York trip but I was getting fat and bored down here. I'll probably end up in the Bowery this trip but as Esperanza used to say I DUNT CARE."

Dear Jack,

    I've read and reread your letter. . . . What's happening, Sweetie? I've heard you say the things you wrote me before— always when something bad was eating away at you.

    I do understand that you need to be alone—and yet not alone, too, I think. But none of that stuff about "importuning," please. I love you and it makes me very happy to be with you, to fry your particular eggs simply because they're your eggs—whether I'm your girl, your mistress, your friend, or whatever—those are all words anyway. I love you quite independently of eighty-six gold rings and documents—don't you understand that, you idiot. So, look—live at Henri's if you think you have to do that now—but the door is still open always. Jack, I don't expect anything from you. Don't be scared of me, please! But I must say I've always thought of you as a Frenchman (Jean Louis Kerouac)—don't think you make a convincing Armenian.

    What's DHARMA BUMS about? Is this the book you wanted to write about Gary Snyder? Will it be finished by the time you come? Today there was something about you in the *Post*—that you'd be at the Vanguard Dec. 24th. I'm glad you're going to be getting a lot of money from it—but I wish you weren't going to do it somehow. . . . It would bug me terribly—I think it would bug anyone except a performer, and a writer is something else entirely. But don't get stage fright—I've always thought you were a damn good reader (you can outread any of those Village actors as Dean Moriarty). Just play it cool, like you said you were going to, pick up your check and walk away—and if you can help it, don't care about whether or not the people liked you. I think you should stay away from the theater, frankly—it's a hollow, rackety, exhausting business (this I *know*) and it's bad enough being involved with it if you're deeply hung up on it, which I don't think you are. Just write your books. All this other business is secondary and simply a way of making a buck. There's some kind of horrible disease in America where it isn't enough to be Jack

Kerouac the writer—but you've got to be Jackie Gleason too, which is fine only if you're Jackie Gleason. Beware! I hope if you do go West afterwards, you'll go because you want to go West, not because you're running from unhappiness in New York—running isn't being free.

I'm all moved into this big, clean apartment now—the nicest place I've lived in—minutes from the Village. It's part of the Village, really—full of painters, writers (young and broke). I'm right near a little Puerto Rican church. Every time I walk by, I hear hand-clapping, tambourines, singing—a kind of new joyful jazz. A little girl danced to "Wake Up Little Susie" in the butchershop. Food is rock-bottom cheap. My friends downstairs* have two cats, which I borrow now and then. My job is deadly, but I come home every night and write, so I don't care much. Maybe I'll be able to quit again in two months when I finish the book. I've had a few run-ins with my boss (who is somewhat like Scrooge before he got hip), but I finally told him I wasn't an office machine and if he persisted in treating me like one, I'd go elsewhere and be treated like a secretary—so he's shut up since and he's even been nice in his unpleasant way. Aside from him, there are some good people there. . . .

Got a letter from Peter. He's trying to find a way to come back without having to pay, but is having trouble finding it. Told me not to worry about Laf, because things are better now that Laf's father is around. But I'll try to see Laf soon anyway—you should have him come see you at the Vanguard. Long mad poem in letter about saints and yogurt by Allen, Gregory and Peter—I'll show you when you come.

Is your mother still coming with you to live in Queens? What're you going to do about finding an apartment?

Playboy announced in back of their Dec. issue "Next month, Jack Kerouac"—if you were wondering about that. Henri's been on the lookout for it, too. Saw him Sunday when he moved me

*The friends were Joan Baker and her husband Leon Prochnik. Leon later worked as the film editor for *Pull My Daisy.*

in. What a sweet guy he is! You're right that he's too good for Fran Evans—although I don't think she's evil, just scared.

Ah, Sweetie, don't be angry. Please believe that an awful lot of people love you. Don't damn everybody like you did in your letter—don't think you mean that anyway.

Love,
Joyce

Part IV

.

December 1957–
March 1958

WHEN JACK RETURNED TO NEW YORK IN DECEMBER, he did indeed move in with Henri Cru, who had helped me move into three different places since July and who lately had seemed particularly friendly to me. He was a big, moon-faced man with an enormous protruding belly, who prided himself on his French cooking. When Jack took me to dinner once at Henri's apartment on West Thirteenth Street, Henri told us that he had spent the whole day making consommé. He became furious when Jack, who was quite drunk, ate little of the feast he had prepared. He always made a great show of being quite exasperated with Jack's lack of common sense. They had known each other since 1939. In the early forties, Henri's girlfriend Edie Parker had fallen for Jack and later married him.

It was forty years before I learned that in late November Henri had written Jack a vicious letter about me, full of words in capitals and dire underlinings, telling him that I was planning a "surprise visit" to Orlando (hardly a surprise since Jack and I had been discussing it in our letters for weeks) and warning him not to get enticed into marriage with a "dog's breakfast": "THE TRAP IS SPRUNG!! DON'T FALL INTO IT!!!!" I suspect Henri Cru wanted Jack all to himself during this period of Jack's celebrity, as a way of aggrandizing his own importance. Perhaps he felt he deserved payback for the loss of Edie or for Jack's comical portrait of him as Remi Boncoeur in *On the Road*. Whatever Henri's motives, the letter must have aroused all Jack's fears of any woman who might demand a full commitment. Distancing himself from me, his thoughts turned again to Helen Weaver. "I want to make it with Helen Weaver," he wrote to Allen Ginsberg and Peter Orlovsky on December 10, suggesting that Peter move in with me in his place.

The first week of Jack's December visit to New York was agonizing for me because I didn't hear from him, even though he was living right across town. I stayed away from Jack's evening of poetry and jazz at the Brata Gallery, which everyone I knew was very excited about. And I was too proud to turn up at the Village Vanguard without an invitation. Jack evidently felt much less comfortable there than at the Brata. Some people said his readings were great, but there were rumors that Jack was drunk for every performance and that the Vanguard had canceled the second week of his engagement. I wasn't surprised. Nothing could have been worse for him than being up on a stage playing the King of the Beatniks night after night. "Harden your heart," my new friend Hettie Jones advised me. But I couldn't. When Jack finally called, inviting me to his second to last performance, I went, taking a seat at one of the darkest back tables.

After a long drumroll, Jack staggered onstage with his head sunk down onto his chest. Before he got started, he turned his back on the audience of collegiate-looking couples and bopped along to the music, waving a bottle of Thunderbird in the air facing the band. Even Zoot Sims and his cool musicians looked embarrassed. When he finally began reading from *On the Road*, he slurred the words, though there were moments when he connected perfectly with the jazz playing behind him. Tears came to my eyes as I watched the place empty out even before Jack was finished.

Backstage, there was a girl hanging around, of course, a nocturnal apparition all in black with dead white makeup. I stepped right in front of her and kissed Jack on the lips. He grabbed me by the shoulders and hung on to me. "Get me out of here," he said.

He and Henri Cru had soon fallen out, so now he was at the

Marlton, the sleazy hotel on Eighth Street, where he'd been stay-ing when I first met him. He passed out on the lumpy double bed and I lay wide awake all night beside him. There was a war going on between pity and love and my anger. In the morning Jack asked me if I'd take him back after his gig at the Vanguard was over.

Sitting at my kitchen table on December 28, he wrote to Allen: "Broke up with Joyce because I wanted to try big sexy brunettes then suddenly saw evil of world and realized Joyce was my angel sister and came back to her."

We spent a week holed up in my apartment with the phone off the hook. Jack slept a lot and tried valiantly not to drink, and we were soon back to our old closeness. We talked about the future, though not our future together. Jack was convinced New York would destroy him, which meant we couldn't live together, as I had been secretly hoping. It would be best for him, he thought, to buy a house somewhere on Long Island and live there with his mother; he would come into the city on weekends to see me and his other friends. I tried to believe that such an arrangement would be enough for me.

By the second week, Jack had recuperated enough to take me to the Hong Fat noodle shop in Chinatown and to the only movie we ever saw together. One day he decided the time had come for us to have a "real date." In the interest of furthering my education, he took me to the Variety Theater on the Bowery, where tickets cost twenty-five cents and the audience consisted of snoring derelicts. We saw *The Sweet Smell of Success* and agreed that the desperate press agent depicted in it, played by Tony Curtis, reminded us of Joe Lustig.

We spent one last weekend together. When I left for my tem-porary job as a typist on Monday morning, Jack was still asleep. A few hours later, Robert Frank, who had been assigned by *Life* to photograph Jack "on the road" in Florida, was going to drive him down to Orlando.

■

Dear Joyce
Gone
on
road,
Robert
finally
woke
me
up
on
phone,
You
are
my
Angel
in
a
pink
slip

Jack "Lax" XXX*

■

I found this note from Jack when I came home from work. It was written in pencil on the back of a yellow flyer from the Brata Gallery on Tenth Street.

Although I didn't realize it, this was the beginning of the end. We'd just had the best days of our entire relationship. Once Jack installed Memere on Long Island, he would never be as tender with me again.

---

*Jack had recently been in correspondence with Robert Lax, a friend of Thomas Merton's and the editor of the Catholic magazine *Jubilee*.

■

[Postcard from Orlando, Florida]
January 10

Dear Joycey . . . Just a note to say that Peter is back in N.Y., as
you may know . . . left LeHavre Jan. 17th S.S. Mauretania . . .
Tell Leo if I buy car twill be a jeepster wagon like Lucien's . . .
Have 3 new offers to make album readings, bigtime companies
too . . . Have finished all my work here and will relax a few weeks
before going to NY, meanwhile write you long letter in few days,
and meanwhile could you send me NYTimes real estate page so I
can study house rentals in outlying areas, I'll rent a house and
spend 3 months looking for proper buy, in NJ or LI, better than
goin in blind. You will help me greatly sending page . . . I buy you
bottle scotch in exchange . . . Finish novel, spit forth finish, be
big rich novelist soon . . . Have happy thoughts, as Allen G's
mother always told me . . . Until

Jack

[Orlando, Florida]
Jan. 13

Dear Joyce, Was more or less waiting for word from you but
I'll write first now. Allen G. says you have a new letter, will you
forward it later? I'm going to send him his money tomorrow, all of
it,* and be done with it and also give him a chance to enjoy
Paris these next 3 months with no worries (unless he gives it
away). I've been very miserable here, my in-laws annoy me no
end, are worse than anybody ever dreamed. The details are too
dreary (& repetitious to my Town & City days when they got
that too.) (The money.) Now I'm wise. In fact I'm leaving this
Fla. and moving to New York. When Steve Allen has me come
up for an album, as he says he'll do, I'll do that then go out on
the Island and find a house to put a down payment on, maybe

*The $225 Allen Ginsberg had advanced Jack in February 1957 for his passage to Tan-
giers.

not so far out as the Hamptons, but someplace or other. But my mother expressly forbids me ever to bring either Ginsberg or Burroughs over to my house, which sounds strange since I'm buying the house and I'm 36 years old. Anyway, may I say I enjoyed our last hours (and weeks) together more than ever. I find you to be the sweetest girl in the world and I want you to know that I respect you for that even love you (as a woman, as a friend, as a anything). Somewhere or other, in the back toilets of nightclubs or bars or in the train toilets, I picked up a dose of crab lice which I'm getting rid of pronto with the proper medication. I might have left some on your toilet seat. If so I'm sorry.— It's raining, gloomy, I told my nephew not to bring his friends around so now the house is full of his friends in a kind of mockery of me in my own house (my mother probably whispers to them that I'm crazy, pay no attention). So I'm locked up in my own room, foolish. At least I can see everything clearly. I sprained my ankle playing basketball and am limping. My supertypewriter (this one) just came in partially repaired (a $27 complete overhaul, they said), the ribbon feeder works but one way and they forgot the "legs" but this is the smoothest typewriter in the world and now I type DHARMA BUMS, big job. I hope Keith and Malcolm like it, if not I'll take it to Hiram. I'm sure Viking will like it . . . It has only one flaw, towards the end, a kind of anticlimax. It doesnt have a mad climactic moment like ROAD. I dunno. But the whole thing is enormously readable, as they say, and in parts sublime, and the end is heavenly. Producer Jerry Wald is writing to me from Hollywood soon. Black Mountain Review is out, by the way, with Allen's AMERICA pome and my instructions on prose and other things, a terrific issue for good old Creeley. (Snyder, Whalen, and above all Burroughs' YAGE (William Lee). I have 2 copies of it, I can give you one when I come to NY.

Send your Elise poem (black leather road) to Rainey Cass, c/o Silver, 18 Cornelia, New York 14 . . . for Climax, the New Orleans Jazz mag, if you want.* Or any other poems you have,

*I never did this—too unsure of myself writing poetry in the Beat vein.

especially jazzy ones. Or even a piece of prose. Leo sent me photos, wild photos, by Jerry Yulsman.*

Ah shit, I feel dreary, I'm telling you there are NO VIBRATIONS in Florida or anywhere in the south, the people are DEAD. Now I'm entering into a period of mingling with human beings again, and leave the quiet night woods a while, I want to be back in the Nation of People, which is New York. I hope Leo or Lucien or Robert or Howard will have time to drive me around L.I. on weekends or something. O yes, Peter is arriving before end of month, Allen says. I gave Peter your new address and phone.

Any more yawks about my vanguard reading, or anything, let me hear of it, Miss Grapevine.

Buy yourself some Petri Port and sit on the rug and play Sid† and light candles. Do you know New York is full of electrical vibrations: that black sweater of mine I sleep in, it always crackles and bristles in New York, here it doesnt.

Mine cats are fine, bigger now, we'll bring them to Long Island and introduce them to snow next December. The other day I went to the supermarket and bought six cans of Calo cat food, a jug of wine, and a bottle of aspirins. The check girls look at me suspiciously. What a dreary place it is, you'd never believe it. I'VE changed, tho, not Florida. I'm for NY again, and so's my mother. Nathless I'll have a quiet hideout in Long Island tho. I've been planning Robt Frank's movie, possibilities of a great French movie are enormous. POET IN NEW YORK, maybe, with Bellamy‡ as Lorca. . . .

In the hassle with my nephew, my mother doesnt want to bug little children, but she did finally quietly tell him to stop upsetting the house and my work room and t'other day the gangs of kids and dogs chased my little kitty across the car-zipping road up

*Yulsman followed Jack around the Village, taking a series of color photos for *Pageant*. One of them, from which I was airbrushed out, was later used for a Gap ad for khakis.
†A reference to the late-night jazz disc jockey Symphony Sid, whom we always listened to together when Jack was in New York.
‡Dick Bellamy, a friend of Frank's, was the director of the Green gallery, an important venue for new artists. He did look like Lorca, but ended up playing the Bishop in *Pull My Daisy*.

a tree which blew my top. What bugs me is that he doesnt obey me but stares at me arrogantly. . . . he is arrogant, indocile, perverse. . . . qualities, my dear, not good for 13 years old. Anyway, I feel like an old Scrooge and you know I'm not an old Scrooge, unless I am really (as Allen may think), I dunno. The movie I'd really like to do is of Henri Cru, Pat MacManus, Keith, Stanley Gould, Leo Garen, Don Allen, Lucien, Helen Elliott and Zev in his room . . . what a vast French movie that would be, A DAY IN NEW YORK. . . . Anyway, I can write that anyway.

When I come back, I'll fly, $5 more, last trip on train I had to pay $1.10 for a seat and got no seat and spent whole trip in toilet. . . . Write! Jack

Joyce, please check phonebook, find me Richard Sheresky's address so I can write to him apologies for being bugged by his friend ("is your book a joke?"). I like Dick.

Thursday, Jan. 14, 1958

Dear Scrooge,

Got your letter and you have mine by now. And here's Allen's letter, which came a few days ago, but writing you from the confusion of the office, I forgot to send it (when it arrived, I saw only my name on it somehow and the red-white-and-blue airmail border and ripped the envelope before I realized it wasn't from you to me). Did Peter put any message in it to me in answer to the letter I wrote him? Does anyone say anything about Lafcadio who just a few minutes ago, amazingly, called me long distance from Northport, asking to speak to you because he thought you were still here (Allen had sent him my number, he said). Laf sounds awfully sad, Jack—he said he'd write you and wanted you to write him (Box 167, Northport, L.I.) He was talking about going to Hollywood and becoming a movie star, said he'd stopped drawing. I hope you'll write him. Maybe I'll see Laf next week—he promised to call me if he came into the city. If he's really interested in acting, I'll introduce him to Leo and Robert. I don't think he wants to see Howard again—said he didn't know Howard. (?)

I'm sad that you're having such a depressing time in Florida—but so happy that you're coming back (it's nice to see you doing what *you* want to do). Will you be coming soon? I have just learned to make barbecued short ribs of beef—simply divine, my dear—and am burning to try them out on you. Aside from that, I just want to see you again. And I've never thought of you as Scrooge, although I called you that tonight in fun . . . and you're perfectly right that some children are little monsters now and then—so don't feel guilty. Even Michael Cook, for whom I babysat last night, has his moments ("Let's play soccer," he says, smiling angelically. "Well . . . okay," say I. "Okay—SOC-CER!" he cries, punching me in the jaw and laughing, etc. etc.) What is one to do?—I think they usually know when they have you any-way, when you're overcome by your sense of them as little kids. You must really stick up for yourself more, I think—I've always felt that about you—other people's feelings are tougher than you imagine most of the time.

Hey, an English publisher, Victor Gollancz, took a 25 pound option on my book—so I'm very happy, but more nervous than ever about finishing (the horror of having my name blackened in England as well as here if I don't). So it's full speed ahead. Symphony Sid continues to uphold me (funny that we both mentioned him with our letters crossing). I think that when I get that $62 or whatever it is, I'll buy an enormous bed at last. Aren't you sick of those little couches that always seem to haunt us?

I haven't heard anything more about the Vanguard. But John Holmes's article is in the Feb. Esquire (did you know?)—I hear it's very fine but haven't seen it yet myself. Also, I saw an advance issue of Playboy which is completely devoted to the Beat Generation—snotty article by Herb Gold, plus two stories about parties in SF and NY beat circles—where your name and Allen's are part of the fictionalized conversation. Strange, no? Things like—"Then there were the Kerouac cats who didn't have any money," etc. People talking about "Have you read HOWL?"

No, you didn't leave any crabs here that I know about.

Tons of snow today—like winters used to be. I have a swollen lip from not ducking a snowball. Joan has a magnificent black eye from somebody's elbow and is wearing dark glasses and looking like a hip child. The super is yelling at his wife (He's forgiven me—was angry mainly at Dick Bellamy and Alfred* who were dueling in the lobby and trying to destroy the radiator—but I assured him *that* would never happen again, which gives me lots of leeway). Wish I could send you a snowball to cheer you up— but all you'd get would be a sad, wet letter. Is your ankle any better? You seem to have had bad luck all the way round this trip. Laf, by the way, was very excited when I told him you might live on Long Island—"Really?" he said, "Really!" I'm sure you'll have lots of drivers—probably a good idea to go with Lucien; somehow I feel he knows everything about houses. . . .

Will you come creeping in with your key in the middle of the night? I'll be waiting . . .

Love,
Joyce

[Postcard from Orlando, Florida]
January 20

Dear Joyce. . . . There was no message in Pete's & Allen's letter . . . in fact Peter aint about to be gone yet and I only rue the fact that I just sent Allen his $225 and he might just pay Pete's fare back with that and be broke again! . . . If you hear from Laf again, ask him what happened to the letter I wrote him in November or, no, December, last month . . . did somebody destroy it? big nice letter. Dont buy a double bed, just a double mattress and lay it on your fine rug in the corner and live like Japanese woman simple. Then with the money you save on a bedstead you buys tea cups and teapots and tea at Bobo's, or another rug, see. Please send me the new VillageVoice attack, I

*The painter Alfred Leslie would later direct *Pull My Daisy*.

want to see it and send it to Allen or somebody. Ankle is better, I'll be able to dance with hip child Joan. Don't send Leon's shirt, I can pick it up next month. Nice gift. I dont feel that my last trip to NY was "unlucky," I still feetl (feel) that I really blew poetry in the club I dont care what anybody else says, never did SOON

Jack

Wednesday, January 22

Dear Jack,

Your card came today, Sweetie, and here is the Village Voice Attack, which I send you but still don't see why you should be bothered—it's quite muddleheaded and actually almost meaning-less, as you'll see, essentially a rehash of [Dan] Wakefield* (how-ever, I understand from Joe L. [Lustig] that [Nat] Hentoff liked ON THE ROAD a lot—but why the Hell doesn't [the writer] say so since that would be relevant information too . . .).

Also, here are the interviews with you and Philip [Lamantia] for the Post, which appeared today and yesterday. You said some very beautiful things. But I do wish—for your own protection and no other reason—that you hadn't admitted to dope. You've really got to start being more discreet when you talk to these newspaper types who of course want as much of a story as they can get, but that's no reason for you to answer any questions they ask you—everyone's entitled to privacy and it's nobody's business whether you smoke Camels or hasheeh. It seems so pointless to stick your neck out for something like this . . . It would be different, I guess, if you wanted to come out with a strong statement about legaliz-ing dope or something . . . Well, even if you said it, it's unforgive-able of [Mike] Wallace to have printed it—he's always struck me as kind of a vulture on TV (a couple of people are sueing him for libel). Steer clear of people like that, they're not Lucien news-

---

*In a piece for The Nation, Wakefield had ridiculed Jack's performance at the Van-guard, calling him an "immature boy poet" and even making fun of the loud shirt he wore.

paper men. It's enough, more than enough, that you make your confessions in your novels as you've done all along. Yes, be like William Faulkner, who carefully misspells his name in the Oxford, Miss. phonebook—"Falkner."

I told Leo you were worried about finding someone to drive you around, and he said that if you'd like to pay $120 to cover the insurance on his old car, which runs fine now, it would be yours—remember, that red convertible? He can't afford its upkeep and would have to pay twice the amount of insurance because he's under 25. But he's going to write you about all this— maybe he's done that already.

Robert's looking forward to the French movie—he said, and I think too, that you should use Joanie in it—what's a French movie sans le danse?

Nothing much has been happening to me because all I do is work and go home and write. I'm very grim about finishing now. Last night, with the aid of Symphony Sid, I solved a major technical horror by eliminating a chapter I used to think I absolutely had to write in which three days passed and nothing happened to the heroine—now I don't understand why this wasn't obvious from the start. Why do I get so hung up just on getting people from one place to another? The other thing I do is cook— strange, exotic dishes with the aid of a cookbook—I'm sick of porkchops for the time being—when you come back, I'll cook you a mad Italian chicken with my burnt fingers, I'll make you Eggs Florentine at 4 A.M.— And I'll get the phonograph fixed for good and all!

Listen, I think you really blew at the Vanguard too—so don't let newspaper crap I send you get you down. I remember especially the way you read those parts from TRISTESSA. . . . A painter I know says that a lot of painters (like Mike Goldberg) are down on you because they feel you're horning in on their territory—writing visually—this, I think, is a big compliment, no? Have you finished typing DHARMA BUMS? Yesterday the Times had a tiny notice about THE SUBTERRANEANS—that it was coming out Feb. 20, and a guy I know picked up an advance copy of it in the Gotham Bookmart, read it straight through immediately and thinks it every bit as good if not better in some ways than ON THE ROAD.

Bobo's???—Explain, please.

How are the orange cats?

Write! Come soon. I love you.

Joyce

[Enclosed newspaper clipping:]

The Real Dope. *In Manhattan. Dishwasher Ping Wing, 72, arrested for possession of narcotics, told police, "I've been on heroin for 55 years, and I've never felt better."*

[Orlando, Florida]
Feb 4 1958

Dear Joyce . . .

Got your letter . . . and the Times section same time, found a nice prospect and wrote to the realtor . . . when I do get a house it will be about 50 miles out and I want to keep the address a secret from the general world including Edw R Murrow . . . like, when I tell you the address, I'll be expecting you to keep it a secret from various mad types [who] are likely on a whim drive out and burst in on my carefully planned solitudes and work schedules, right? Lucien is mad but I wouldnt mind Lucien my best friend busting in, but but . . . there are too many hipsters looking for me. One of them, you know, Bob Donlin, keeps sending me elaborate expensive telegrams from Cafe Riviera telling me he's dead broke and needs money immediately . . . I dont even answer, letting him think I'm gone from Florida . . . he did this to Allen, too, last year, and Allen sent him $40 . . . it could go on forever . . . I can just see him cashing the telegram money order and buying drinks for the house . . . Meanwhile, Henri has written me a rather nasty letter, in a way, that is, complaining because I showed up at his house with a "97 cent tokay bottle" and his girl June says I made him out a louse in On the Road, etc.

so I've ceased to bother answering all such twaddle &
foolishness . . . just because I'm going to be rich doesnt mean I
dont stick to my good old 97 cent tokay, too. . . . In fact, in fur-
nishing my new house, I'm going to go down to Delancey Street
or old shoppes in the country and buy nothing but beat up old
furniture, I want a happy ramshackle type home, that was my
dream in the beginning . . . old round mission wood tables, old
easy chairs, old square back piano, an old rolltop desk huge like
Leo's, etc. etc. Actually I hope movies buy because if they dont
I'll be hungup with that house, the monthly payments anyway to
be guaranteed by my mother's social security but what about food
if my "boom" ends? I dont think it will end, tho, too many new
manuscripts in the works . . . I keep turning it out, they keep taking it, that's the way Hugo and Zola made it, and Balzac. Allen is
mighty lucky his father's going to leave him a house, Allen
doesnt put out enough work . . . like you say, yes, a travel article
about Europe. —When I mentioned Bobo's in a recent letter, I
meant that chinese restaurant we went to, you should buy a
pound of that wonderful tea they serve, if you want real tea— I'll
be in NY in 3 or 4 weeks, maybe 4, making my date for a Steve
Allen album, he's already advanced more than my fare, and I'm
going to make other albums too.—I don't understand the [Ken-
neth] Rexroth* item in NYTimes, 'pears like Rexroth still wants
to grab off the "beat generation" as his own invention & baby
and you watch, he'll end up trying to turn it to politics and start
rumors everywhere, I dont like him, and I dont trust him, and I
wrote 2 weeks ago and told him I was disassociating myself from
his sphere of interests and he didnt reply altho the rest of the letter was friendly (by "interests," I meant political shit). I'm going
to take very great care to stay out of sight of that old raging fud.
Anarchist indeed. I guess you dont have to send any more
NYTimes, it'll be better for me to show up at the realtors in their
locales. Keith Jennison can drive me up to the country too, and I

*An older, well-established San Francisco poet, who was quite jealous of the attention
Jack and Allen had been given. He came to New York for a poetry and jazz appearance
at the Five Spot that winter to defend his turf.

have an in-law in Jersey, and can go to L.I. with Howard or Robert Frank. No errands, just whatever you hear . . . for instance last Sunday on the TV show the Last Word with Garry Moore, John Mason Brown and moderator whatizname they discussed the word "beat" and me and my book at great length and I didnt even see it or know it, just heard about it. . . . Same with something about me in Newsweek about 2 or 3 weeks ago or maybe have you seen, heard? can find? It doesn't really matter, like Faulkner I dont care any more and as for Joe Lustig I wont bother with bits & patches of hope any more, I'm back in my starry element. I'm sending a nice prose piece about Buddhism from Dharma Bums to Chicago Review, the last chapter of Doctor Sax to Gregory Corso for German publication (in German langue) and Lucien Midnight I'm typing up for anybody (since it's been lost). . . . Allen is very happy in Paris, got his money, Burroughs turned sweet & friendly instead of scarey (to him) and they went on a week jaunt to London I hear to see the angry young men who I imagine are a bunch of screaming fairies from the sound of it, English literature being what it is (literatera?) literateurs? "I'm just so *angry!* I could just b-i-t-e the mall . . . I could djus sit and pee . . . . (lisp) . . . I mean, dearie, I'm jus so m-a-d. . . ." I'm living nice life now, playing my solitaire baseball game, which is a beautiful thing, you'll see it, and doing my work, and cats, and full-moon nights in my yard, and occasional home drunks, and good food, and much sleep & universal prayer. By universal prayer I simply mean, when I step out of the house and look up at those cloudy worlds of stars, it becomes awfully easy to feel compassion that this dream can be so sad & mistaken, you know what I mean . . . mere thought is a prayer,

> dont worry I wont drag you
> to church with Billy Graham
> Write soon,
> Jack

Dear Jack,

I've been wanting to answer your letter before this, but I got sick again—this time kind of a strep throat and a temperature of 104 1/2 degrees—and my father kidnapped me from here in a taxi, very dramatic ride to 116th Street wrapped up in blankets coughing and spitting à la Camille with poor Dad wringing his hands—but I survived after all, though I didn't get to a typewriter till now, the first day I'm back, and I didn't want to inflict my ekhelhoptic unreadable handwriting on you. . . . So you're really coming back, eh? It's nice to see you talking about "realty" and "prospects"—you have definitely become an homme d'affaires (is that how you say it?), suddenly you have grown a very good cigar and are surrounded by old brandy bottles (bottles of old brandy, rather) but I'm glad too you haven't forgotten your old Tokay and to hell with Henri Cru for his pettiness, even though he is very nice,* I guess—he does have this obsessed thing about him, I've noticed it before. What's this nice prospect you mention? If you want me to start sending the Times again, just yell. Are you having good weather in Florida? I heard it was freezing there. Are you winning at solitary baseball?—do explain it to me someday, but I warn you now that I have always been incredibly stupid about all balls—base, basket, foot, etc.—never could catch except by somehow getting the ball locked under chin with my knee up in the air (if you can imagine that!), my father gave up on me long ago.

I like your idea of a comfortable, ramshackle house. I've never liked those arranged sorts of rooms where everything matches and nobody ever leaves any imprint unless there's an accident. I hope you'll get your round table and lamp in the kitchen at last. I know a place in the Village that sells old country-style furniture and is very cheap. The lower East Side is better for little things

---

*I still had no inkling that Henri Cru had warned Jack against me; Jack had never mentioned his letter.

like dishes, gadgets, and linen. Now your return has started to be real. I've always been convinced until you were in the door that you'd never get here and have always felt I'd never see you again when I saw you off, which is why I wept (which you've never liked, I know. I guess you prefer to see the end of a place by yourself, but I always felt I couldn't bear not to see the last of you—and I won't apologize either.) Also, I always used to half dread your coming, because it meant the beginning of your going away and every moment that you were here seemed terribly fraught somehow, painful . . . I've never had such a sense of the rush of time, and yet the weeks that you were here seemed very, very long, and when I was alone again, it seemed as if I'd been away for a year. Strange . . . And now it will be different—there'll be more ease between us, I think. It was different last time too, already, I think you felt it—the end of a kind of desperate hung-upness in me . . . or maybe I'm just getting older. I've begun to feel older of late, no longer think of everybody else as adults. Well, I wonder what you think of all this . . . I used to doubt whether you knew anything about me . . . but now I think perhaps you've known everything all along . . . didn't think you were as wise as you are until I read THE SUBTERRANEANS, where your perfect knowledge of yourself and everything around you shook me up and astounded me.

I'm enclosing some items from last week's Village Voice, which should interest you, particularly Anton Rosenberg's letter. I am afraid I wasn't exactly au courant last week and so didn't hear about anything else. No, I didn't know about the TV or Newsweek—will look up the latter for you, if I can. Do you understand H. B. Lutz's article?—I think he's sending up a half-hearted, equivocal cheer for the Beats, but what's he doing in all the other paragraphs? Tell Allen to write about THE ANGRY YOUNG MEN—that would be a hot article topic. Very wise of you to now dissociate yourself from any definite group—stick to it—especially if you meet any press people. Groups are mainly invented to make things easy for overworked critics anyway. It's depressing to see how a lot of bad writers have now picked up on what they think is a Beat style—went to a poetry reading, where poems by five poets were all greyly alike, hip language already solidified into cliche by lack of imagination. I said so and received angry looks. There's never been so much poetry and such bad poetry—from both sides. So it can't really be called a "Poetic Renaissance" just a period of "mass poetic activity" or something. And I'm not being snobbish. You come back and see what I mean. . . . Hey, every time I turn on the radio or TV, I hear the word "Beat"—example: Doctor in TV drama coming out of operating room, having performed crucial transplant of someone's kidney that four lives depend upon with drunken intern assisting—well, what do you think he says?—"Man, I'm beat, beat, beat. I'm beat."

That's all for now. I've got to go back to novel—felt too lousy to do anything on it all week. Take care, Sweetie and write soon.

Love,
Joyce

P.S. Of course, I won't tell anyone your address.
P.S. Can't imagine why I didn't remember Bobo's. Now I'll make pilgrimage and buy tea. We will sit on my carpet and drink it with one red candle burning for luck.

Joyce

February 12, 1957

Dear Dorothy,*

This is my new address: 338 East 13th Street, NYC. I've been here since December. It's an apartment between 1st and 2nd Avenue, 2 rooms, very modern and amazingly cheap, the first place I've had that really seems like my home rather than just my apartment. My parents flipped weakly about the neighborhood which they consider completely déclassée ("What we spent years getting away from, *you* had to go back to," etc.), but they have

---

*Dorothy Sucher, my first cousin and good friend, lived in Maryland.

actually showered me with all sorts of household goods (so that I won't let "my standards" go) . . . in fact they've been downright lovely, and I possess at last a Peruvian rug, gourds, candlesticks, a toaster, and so on. And I dig the Lower East Side! Always did. Am living on bagels and herring. Right next door, there's an organization called the Jaguar Sewing Club Center, and across the street, a sign reading JESUS SANA Y SALVA hangs on an ex-Synagogue. How's that for local color? Also, a friend I've had ever since High School lives in the same house—I took her apartment when she and her husband moved into a larger one.

My book is, alas, not coming out this spring but next fall at the earliest. I'm still working on it. I've been held up by all sorts of things like Jack Kerouac, economic insecurity, 2 attacks of the flu and plain hung-upness—but I'll finish it now if it's the last thing I do.

I'm not married. I'm not engaged. Jack has come and gone twice and in 3 weeks is coming back permanently to live in a house on Long Island with his mother. I don't know yet how *she* will affect the situation. I hear she likes me (never having met me), but calls me La Glassman (which sounds ominous). And Jack is lovely but quite mad which one just has to accept since there's no hope that he'll ever be otherwise so I really don't know what's going to happen, don't even know what I'd want if I had to make my mind up. Part of me feels like running off to Europe or someplace anyway! Meanwhile I guess I'm "going steady" in a sort of nervous, unspoken arrangement that goes on and on with no particular end in sight—if you know what I mean. Lots of letters back and forth—Like Peter Ilyich Tchiakowsky and whoever that woman was. It's even more domestic than romantic—when we're together, most of the time we talk about what we're going to have for dinner, when we do talk. Curiously enough, this satisfies me more than any other relationship I've had. I'm not unhappy.

I have a job working odd hours for a press agent who's quite a bit like the press agent in that movie THE SWEET SMELL OF SUCCESS. I think he's disintegrating. He keeps saying, "I'm going off my skull, Sweetie." Also his checks bounce and one day a blonde and two cops came looking for him. So I've started to look for another job out of the corner of my eye, but am actually not too disturbed. Don't care what I do jobwise anymore. I've come to feel like a writer, which is ruinous financially.

Well, that's as much of a summary as I'll bore you with. Do write again, Dorothy, and I promise to be a faithful correspondent hereafter. I have missed you and often think of you. It's simply been a case of lack of ertia or something.

Love,
Joyce

[mid-February 1958]
Sunday

Dear Jack,

Spring today and a stiff wind and a late afternoon moon just now that looks like the moon in Henri Rousseau paintings. The Times real estate section is on its way to you now in a separate envelope. It's funny somehow to think of you in Florida reading it. I promise to send it every week till you come. Before I got your card, I'd half expected you to come rolling in sometime this week. Yes, I knew Peter was back because he called me but I haven't seen him yet—he said he'd see me once he had a job, so I guess he's still without one, he sounded blue.

I am typing this with new records on the phonograph—went mad yesterday and bought 2 lps—one a Vivaldi concerto for two trumpets which you will love. It's very much like jazz, with the trumpets cutting through the strings like knives. Also a Bud Powell record which I'm getting used to. Do you like him? Nothing much of interest has been happening to me, except that things are getting rocky with Joe Lustig. His paychecks to me are beginning to have a nasty habit of bouncing, which means that my checks bounce too, and this is a drag. Besides which, he is kind of a drag. I guess I really don't like him. He's a real opportunist-hustler hanging on to the coattails of the arts—and he's not even very good at it. For God's sake, don't ever let him con you into getting involved with him in any business way. There's really *nothing* he can do. So . . . I guess I'll be looking for a regular job again, though maybe not till I finish the book. I've never been so completely uninterested in having a job—and with that attitude it's not so easy to find one, since they expect you to come on enthusiastic and bright-eyed. Nevertheless, I do seem to be thinking happy thoughts or calm no-thoughts (I'm always a bit suspicious of feeling happy), but anyway, I just drift along pleasantly enough and whenever a check bounces I remark, "Oh, a check bounced," and don't feel one way or the other about it. . . . Strange.

Joan, on the other hand, is going through a period of ecstatic hepped-upness, so much so that she can't bear to go to bed, stays up all night and gets thinner, higher, and more exhausted by the day, and is constantly dancing, even in her sleep. We sit up night after night drinking Russian tea in a glass with raspberry jam in it, giggling at each other and planning fantastic ballets. I have gone with her to see a lot of dance lately—most of it is pretentious and dull, but somehow it's making me discover very definite aesthetic principles inside me, which I never knew I possessed. I wish you had been with me at Cooper Union one night, when they had five dancers on stage answering questions from the audience after they'd performed—most of them went on and on with all kinds of lengthy earnest shit about how in order to dance you had to have time, motion and a body, etc. etc., but one guy, Jimmy Waring (the only one whose work had been at all exciting) answered everything in a curt Zen way, saying: "I just dance, I just move. And yeah, I think it takes two to communicate . . ." Well, it was much better than that, and I can't remember it, damn it.

There's a clipping from today's Book Review section in this letter. Also, the Mike Wallace interviews were rehashed in Time Magazine's Religion section (did you know?) and a big picture of Philip Lamantia was printed—I was told about this, didn't see it. Also, the Saturday Review of Lit. had something in it about

Allen, Peter and Gregory invading Brentano's in Paris and trying to get them to sell the Evergreen Review and getting kicked out—I didn't see this one either . . . And someone told me that a book to be entitled something like ENGLAND'S ANGRY YOUNG MEN AND OUR BEAT GENERATION is to come out this summer. Seems to me that every time I open a newspaper or magazine, there's mention of you, Allen, or the Beat Generation—you could probably coast along from now on without ever doing another interview. I bet if Allen wrote some kind of article on how he digs Europe, he could get it published and live for a couple of months on the proceeds. I met a Doubleday editor at a party who's going to Europe this spring and seemed interested in looking Allen up.

I read your article on writing in the Black Mountain review and got so wound up, I sat down and wrote half a chapter before I knew what I was doing. But this happens rarely, rarely.

Lemme know if you've got any other errands and I'll do what I can.

Love,
Joyce

Part V

.

April-August, 1958

J ACK RETURNED TO NEW YORK IN EARLY MARCH, determined to
find a house on Long Island as soon as possible. It was then that
I suggested Northport. Robert Frank drove us out there one day
and Jack bought the second house he saw, a brown-shingled house
overlooking a high school football field. The realtor who showed
us around was thrilled at the prospect of having such a celebrity in
Northport and rattled off the names of artistically inclined people
Jack would absolutely have to meet. She seemed to take it for
granted that Jack and I were an engaged couple. "And here's the
nursery!" she sang, throwing open the door to a small sunlit bedroom.

Jack and I stood there in silence. I wondered if Jack was as
aware of the painful irony of this moment as I was. I remember the
downcast feeling I had the rest of the afternoon, although Jack was
very excited and couldn't wait to tell his mother about the house
he'd bought for her.

Shortly before he returned to Orlando to start packing, he went
out one night with Gregory Corso to the Kettle of Fish, a bar on
MacDougal Street that had a rough clientele and was frequented
by moving men like Henri Cru. In the fall Jack and I had been
photographed in front of its red neon sign by Jerry Yulsman. In the
small hours of the morning, Jack and Gregory left the bar, followed
outside by two men, who beat Jack up, banging his head repeatedly

against the curb and breaking his nose and his arm. To his horror, he found he lacked the will to defend himself. Gregory brought Jack home to me with blood running down his face, and we made him go with us to a nearby hospital. "Cauterize my wounds," he kept saying.

"Was drunk 2 weeks ago," he wrote to Philip Whalen from his new house in Northport in mid-April, "got beat up by hoodlums, stopt getting soused, feel great . . . sobriety is really an absorbing contemplation. Have changed a little, tho. No joy. No sorrow needer."

Although the doctors in the emergency room at the New York Infirmary had assured Jack he did not have a concussion, he would later believe he had suffered brain damage that night and that afterward he had never been the same. "Maybe once I was kind drunk," he reflected in a letter to Allen Ginsberg in March 1959, "but am now brain-clogged drunk with the kindness valve clogged by injury."

I felt the immediate effects of Jack's beating by his marked withdrawal. New York was an evil place where everyone—from critics to barflies to old friends—was out to destroy him, a view his mother, intent on keeping Jack at home with her in Northport and separating him from bad influences like Burroughs and Allen Ginsberg, also espoused. Since Jack associated me with his New York life, he rapidly began distancing himself from me as well as his other friends in the city.

I didn't hear much from Jack until late April, after he and Memere had settled into their house. The one weekend Jack came into New York, he made it clear to me that from now on he would be spending most of his time on Long Island.

During our weekend, I'd suggested that Jack write a novel about everything that had happened to him in the past year—the whole awful, overwhelming experience of becoming famous. He sent me a penny postcard saying he was seriously thinking about it; he'd call it *Fame in America*—we were always trying titles out on each other. (Jack didn't write this book until 1961, changing its title to *An American Passes Through*; a couple of years later, desperate enough for money to follow a misguided suggestion from his latest editor, Ellis Amburn, he would combine it with the previously written *Desolation Angels*. The two stylistically different halves of the resulting book proved to be an awkward fit. Shortly before his death in 1969, Jack began to write another novel about the same devastating period of his life. He called it *The Spotlight* and left it unfinished.)

As spring turned into summer, Jack began communicating with me mostly through penny postcards,* directing me to take care of various things for him. Since he had no phone in his house and had to walk half a mile to the nearest phone booth, calls from him were a rarity; he also considered them a waste of thirty-five cents.

■

[early May 1958]
Wednesday

Dear Jack,

Thanks so much for sending such a fast check—$15 was exactly what you owed me. No, you didn't say $100, I didn't expect it, and would have sent it straight back embarrassed.

Yes, FAME IN AMERICA is the right title, I think (although, what about AMERICAN FAME?) Say, you're really going to write that book, aren't you? Are there any things that you've blacked out on that maybe I remember? Let me know.

I'm sorry you felt so depressed about New York once you reached home. But, Baby, forgive me for being boring, but I do think it's all that drinking—not drinking itself but the *amount of it* you do. Like my cats, you don't know when to stop. It's really desperate, gluttonous drinking—like maybe the whiskey ocean's going to dry up soon, which, alas, it won't, you know. Listen, when you come to NY in October, why don't you try this?—eat a really good meal somewhere, with maybe a glass of wine or two, and then just stick to beer. It was those two bottles of wine that

*Most of these cards have been lost.

fouled you up. Also, to avoid feeling shabby, bring one clean shirt and pajamas next time—horrible feeling living in same clothes for three days, sordid, my dear. Oh, practical bourgeois Joyce that I am, don't let me bug you, but consider above suggestions. *Also,* don't you know after thirty-six years that all the bars are always crowded with people who never take their eyes off the door because they are waiting hopefully for the Messiah to come walking in any minute, expecting revelation, God-knows-what, the final conversation—when the only Messiah is the person on the barstool next to you sometimes when you stop looking at the door for a moment. So, Sweetie, here you came Friday night furiously seeking, when there was just old sweet Allen all the time, Lucien, Robert—how many people can you know well anyway, how many people can you really love? I think you actually accomplished what you wanted in New York, though you won't admit it, but maybe you will in memory. Oh, don't know what I'm talking about here, so will stop. YES! Write that book about last year—I think you need to see you haven't stopped having things happen to you, I think there is only comfort in form for people like us, the sudden bright seeing that nothing is wasted or to be regretted, not even suffering, not even one's mistakes. If I weren't able to see form now and then, I wouldn't want to be alive.

Ah well. . . .

Be as kind to yourself as you are to your cats—and I want you to know you made me awfully happy last weekend and I wish I could make you awfully happy, or that something could.

Love,
Joyce

DHARMA BUMS very beautiful!

■

One Saturday morning in late May, armed with a big loaf of black pumpernickel, which Jack had asked for, I set out for Northport on the LIRR. To make a good impression upon Memere,

I'd put on one of my secretarial outfits, a flowered cotton shirtwaist dress, and rolled up my long, straight hair into a French twist—I could pass for a nice bourgeois girl if you didn't know my history. I wasn't very sure of my welcome. It felt like ages since Jack and I had been together. I was the one who had proposed the visit, and he had agreed to it, in a few curt words on one of his postcards.

I wasn't expecting to stay overnight; Jack had made it clear to me that his mother would not permit an unmarried couple to sleep together under her roof. He wasn't going to meet me at the station either but he had given me directions on how to get to his house. I was to board a bus after I got off the train.

Sure enough, a bus was waiting. I took a seat by a window and watched the other passengers get on—a lot of gray-haired people, each one carrying a package or a shopping bag. The bus turned onto a highway and I was surprised when we kept going without making any stops; nothing we passed reminded me of anything I'd seen on my previous visits to Northport with Howard. Finally the bus rolled through the gates of what at first looked like a country estate, and all the other passengers got off. When I looked out the window, I saw men wandering around on a big lawn with shuffling steps, gesticulating and talking to themselves. The bus had carried me into the grounds of a vast mental hospital. I remember feeling quite shaken, as if ending up here by mistake somehow prefigured what I would find when I saw Jack.

It took me another hour to arrive at the house. Memere greeted me at the door with a blunt, inhospitable question: "What train are you going back on?" She was a grandmotherly figure in her house-dress and apron—short and squat, with thick round glasses and iron-gray hair pulled into a bun. She told me she had been cooking since early that morning. As I entered the house, I could smell meat roasting in the kitchen. A heavy meal was being prepared even though it was a hot summer day.

The house I'd seen two months before was no longer empty. The downstairs—Memere's domain—was filled with the kind of orangey maple furniture with plaid upholstery one might find in a Sears, Roebuck catalog. You would not think the writer who was the avatar of the Beat Generation lived there. A picture of the Virgin Mary hung in the kitchen.

Jack seemed glum and dispirited and, to my great disappointment, already drunk at two in the afternoon. I had hoped that in his hermit life, he'd be able to cut down on alcohol. Interrupting my stiff conversation with Memere, he told me he wanted me to see his study and took me upstairs. It was the room he'd always dreamed of having, with a good typewriter and bookshelves and file cabinets. He could look out and watch football practice on the playing field of the high school next door. All his manuscripts were in the files, he told me proudly, not only the ones like *On the Road*, which he called his "boogs," but others he referred to mysteriously as his "novels" (I've always wondered what those novels were). He showed me the manuscript of *Dharma Bums* and sat there drinking wine as I read the opening pages. He hadn't touched me since I'd walked into the house, and when I tried to kiss him, he stood there unresponsively, then backed away. "We can't do that here," he said sternly. "I told you." His mother kept calling to him, "Jackie! Jackie!" while we were up there in his room. Sometimes he would ignore her, sometimes he would walk to the stairs and ask her what she wanted.

Suddenly I became aware of a commotion outside. Two convertibles full of teenagers had pulled into the driveway, and they all piled out and banged on the door. To my surprise, Memere was quite willing to let them in. (Perhaps they were no threat to her, unlike the unwelcome young woman from the city.) They poured into the living room as we came downstairs. They were rich kids, high school seniors, all suntanned and confident and dressed for the beach, like kids in those beach blanket movies, and they wanted to whisk Jack off to a party at some house on the Sound. "Come on, Jack. Let's go, go, go, man," they said, in their Northport version of Beatnik argot. Jack was laughing and blearily shaking his head. Two seventeen-year-old girls seized his hand and led him out of the room like a child. "You can come, too," they said to me. "There's room in the car." The last thing I felt like doing was going to their party, but I said good-bye to Memere and went with them. It seemed like everything was out of my hands now, the way I'd felt on the bus as it bore me inexorably along to the wrong destination.

All I remember about the party is a room—a huge white room with white furniture and a wall of windows looking out onto blue water. It was a room that reminded me of all the money neither Jack nor I would ever have, and I hated it. It was paradise, really, though all these Northport kids seemed restless for something very different. There was an orange shag rug and the girls that surrounded Jack stood barefoot on it in their bathing suits, and I hated their long brown legs. "You're the saddest man I've ever known," a dark-haired girl with a sensitive face said to Jack, gazing into his eyes. Later she asked me where I lived and seemed impressed by the fact that I had my own place. "How do you find an apartment in Greenwich Village?" she wanted to know, as if she were taking notes so that she could move there herself in a few more years. I said I had no idea.

By the time we were driven back to Jack's house, Memere had put an enormous amount of food on the table—brown, claustrophobic food in thick sauces, steaming hot—enough to feed several other guests. She piled meat and potatoes on Jack's plate, and was upset that he ate none of it, though he steadily drank the wine she put in front of him. After a while he put his head down on the table and closed his eyes. "You see—he doesn't eat," she said to me in a despairing voice. I felt so sad, I didn't know what to say.

I helped Memere clear the table and volunteered to do the dishes. This was a great mistake. She didn't approve of the way I washed dishes at all. "You're wasteful," she told me angrily. "You use too much hot water." It was as if all the dark suspicions she'd had about me were now confirmed by my profligate New York way of washing dishes. "Don't you have to get your train?" Memere finally asked me, even though it wasn't due for another couple of hours. She shooed me out of her kitchen, and I went back to the dining room, where Jack was still passed out with his head on the table.

I roused him to ask if he'd come to the station with me, which was my only hope of seeing him alone, but he wanted to stay where he was and I got tearful.

Soon after, I left for the station by myself.

■

June 3, 1958

Dear Jack,

How are you, Sweetie? Is your hand better? What's happening in Northport? The great Summer exodus from the city has now begun—painters, poets, the Franks . . . the cats have now discovered the joys of the window sill and have sooty faces . . . John the Bartender gives out free drinks to everyone in the Cedar . . . but it's getting quieter and quieter. Lucien and Cessa have produced another little boy—this one is named Ethan (the three New England Karamazovs: Simon, Caleb,* and Ethan). My cousin seems to name her children after angels (Gabriel and Michael). Lucien, by the way, keeps asking me when he's going to see you. It's hard for him to make it out to Northport on account of the baby, but he might later this week and will write you anyhow. What are the chances for you coming in this week? I am waiting for you behind the barn . . . si tu comprends ca? If you don't come in, I shall come out Saturday and visit you (okay?), bringing another pumpernickel, or possibly an onion rye, and your mother wanted me to get her an Italian coffee-pot. Give my regards to her, by the way. I shall also this time bring you SENTIMENTAL EDU-CATION, and I want to finish Dharma Bums. Leon [Prochnik] gave me a letter to send you since now he's spoken to his boss,† so you'll get it when you get this. Also, here are some Times clippings—I think V. S. Pritchett rather appreciates you, which is a refreshing change.

Last weekend I finally went on a "big trip"—which was to Maryland to see my cousins. Against your advice, I took the

---

*Later to become the best-selling author of *The Alienist*.
†About Jack writing a short film for TV. Leon's boss produced TV commercials.

bus . . . very uncomfortable, but I don't regret it . . . what a weird feeling it was, especially at night, like being dead, somehow, with the dark void all around me—what I mean is, I didn't want to ever get off, couldn't even imagine that the bus would ever actually stop, so there I'd be in my seat for eternity, neither still nor moving, with nothing ever happening to me—I was curiously happy that way. Have you ever felt that buses don't seem like buses but more like dark private tubes funnelling you through the U.S.? Also, the solitude of the bus seat is another strange thing— even if a soldier is sitting next to you madly offering you cigarettes, you're still alone and immune . . . and after a while all the strangers fall asleep side by side, some touching, completely unconscious of one another—that's strange, isn't it? I like the busdrivers—all dashing Southern gentlemen, the ones I met up with. After mine had made his little speech about stopping along the way so people could use the john, a lady called out, "Say, Mister, could you-all tell me your name, so's I could tell my sister?"

Washington disappointed me. I thought, "Here I am in the nation's capital," and expected to see a few of the Seven Wonders of the World at least . . . but the White House is small and the city itself is just like Brooklyn, except that it has more trees and a higher concentration of palmistry shops. No, I'm being a little unfair—it has places like the Corinthian Baptist Church and the beautiful banks of the Potomac (which I hear is a great vice pick-up scene, true?). Well, for the first time in my life anyway, I did get some sort of sense of America—American awfulness and sadness, mainly, I'm afraid, like little Negro towns in Maryland with 25 dingy loan offices on Main Street and 2 groceries, and people roaming around in cars with no place to go, and most of the free space I saw disfigured by cars and Coca-Cola signs and too many gas stations all waving silly colored flags—but maybe that's just where I was—Virginia, across the Potomac, looked impossibly green. I think I would like the real wilderness, like tops of mountains and middles of forests, and would know *why* I had gone there rather than stay in the city—but not these frightened dreary towns! How different Northport is, though, or places like Cherry Plains*—so I guess the town scene isn't all that bad—I'd just swallowed too much of that "Let's get away from it all to Podunk and start anew" philosophy—to be found in many cheap novels.

Well, Kerouac, I've stolen half an hour from Hawthorn Books and must now get back to work. Next time I see you, I shall tell you all my perilous adventures . . .

Au revoir,

Love,
Joyce

P.S. If you come into town Friday, maybe you'd call me at the office and let me know (the number's on this stationery). I don't always go home right after work.

■

I had tried to write a newsy, jaunty letter, although I was still feel-ing quite upset by my trip to Northport. But I was game to try again, even though I was not looking forward to it. Wouldn't Jack realize sooner or later that this suffocating life with his mother would never work for him? I was afraid that if I couldn't visit North-port from time to time, we would begin to lose each other.†

I'd gone to see my cousin Dorothy Sucher in Maryland because I felt I couldn't spend one more weekend in my lonely apartment with the gray dust seeping in from the airshaft window. It felt very strange, almost surreal, to visit a normal married couple in a hous-ing development, to help Dorothy fold diapers and accompany her to the most gigantic supermarket I'd ever seen. This was an Amer-ica I knew nothing about and that knew nothing about me. Sitting

---

*Where Lucien Carr had the country house we'd visited.
†"I'm retired from the world now," Jack would write Allen Ginsberg by July, "and going into my mountain shack later and eventually just disappear in woods as far as it can be done these days. Thats why I've made no effort to see poor Peter or even Joyce any-more."

on the Greyhound on my way back to New York, I realized that after all my ambitious plans for transcontinental travel, this was the "on the road" experience I'd ended up with.

■

Dear Joyce

Will be in town fairly soon to sign contracts of movie sale of Road, which you may've seen annoncez in the new york times. The sales price piddling,* less than dennis murphy,† but I will pay [for] the house, furnish it, put rest in bank at 3¼ percent for taxes, and write only what I want, blow as deep as I want, and be a good honest bum again. (Like when I had no money at all.) So, and no more bull like Life Mag and John Wingate and crap bazaar argosy mademoiselle and esquire. On reading holmes' book closely I have no statement to make about it. I have a list of letters an arm long to answer and suddenly I realized I wont answer them at all—silence is not a rebuke, and it expresses my desire to be left alone to work now. In connection with that, my mother and I have (rightly) decided, following Knowles'‡ recent weekend, to cut out all weekending altogether (except relatives like her sister and daughter) because it always ends up with her being bothered all weekend with extra meals and extra linen etc. and what is this if it isnt a home? not a hotel. So I told her I'd separate my own life from the life in her house, and go see my friends in NY instead of having them come out. Knowles was the last

---

*Sterling Lord had previously refused an offer for $100,000, feeling it wasn't big enough.
†Dennis Murphy, a young Viking author Jack and I had met in the fall, had published a very well received first novel, The Sergeant, and sold it to the movies.
‡John Knowles had come to Northport to interview Jack for the Saturday Evening Post.

straw, he was sposed to take us to lobster dinner and preferred
instead another of my ma's homecooked meals. He was nice, all
went well, but goddamit he kept following me around from room
to room, I'm sick of all this attention I dont want. I'm going to
have to tell him, too; in fact did, already, mention it, to his great
chagrin. I like him but the list is too long of people I really like
but that only disturb the tender routines of what is after all an
elderly lady. So please dont come out any more Joyce, I'll see you
in NY, real soon, next week I guess. I think this is the right idea
and not only for my mother's comfort in her own home, but to
make this place my haven for work. My record shows Saturday
my best worknight. Got a card from Robt., I wish he didnt me
blame for the Life rejection, I did my best, not that he blames me
but he seems disappointed in me about something. I'll see him.
We'll do something or other, but it's only personal, I dont need
any more goddam magazine money and trouble. My last magazine
is Holiday, which takes far-out prose and at the same time pays to
send you on trips: first trip to Quebec, in July, expense account,
article will be worth $1500 if they take it. But all other magazines
go fuck. In other words when Time comes to this house in Sept.
I'm going to throw them off the porch. Pretty soon I'll have as
much money as Dennis, too. My hand only now slowly healing to
normal, I discovered the sore spot in the WRIST . . . doctors
didn't detect nothin. When I come in to see you I want to get a
Proust trade for those nowhere books* and also will you try to get
bennies from your doctor for late night work, I'll pay you. And
we'll have a good time. soon

Jack

*A reference to the novels publishers had been sending him with requests for blurbs.

Dear Joyce

Will you please forward this to Hiram Haydn,* I just dont
have the random house address.

Be sure to not overlook this . . . the statement is good for him.
Also you can write Haydn a note while you're at it telling him
about the state of your novel.

I had to go to NY the other day mad as a hatter to contest
Viking's shitty idea of making as much as 4000 corrections on
Dharma Bums. They said copy-editing hadnt hurt ROAD but
that was a short-sentence style that couldnt be hurt. They agreed
first to start all over again, I told them at my expense too, to
prove to them I meant it, now after I'm back home they start to
hedge and want me to go over the galleys and make my 4,000
restorations to the original (hardly any room in the margins) and
finally now the damn galley aint arrived in the mail from them
and if they are trying to sneak over their ersatz version of DB on
me they've lost a writer.

They sorta laffed at me, not really understanding what I tried
to explain about prose . . . they spoke about their "house style"
and such sickening crap. Tom G.† was not disturbed at all and
looked to me like it suited him, but Helen T.‡ doesnt seem
pleased at all, I really let her have it, the speeches. . . . Sterling
was sitting behind me. While all this was going on he got a call
from MGM in Hollywood, they take out small option on subterraneans and if buy, give 15 g's (not much but completely unexpected). Meanwhile Jerry Wald writes me he's disappointed I
didn't sell Road to HIM! crazy. So I have to correct galleys now,

---

*Jack had relented and was writing Haydn about Holmes's novel *The Horn*.
†Thomas Guinzburg was the head of Viking.
‡Helen Taylor had done much of the line editing on *Dharma Bums* as well as on *On the Road*.

when they get here, and rest up from the 2 day binge I went on, calling Leon [Prochnik] 5 million times and he was never in and just as I suspected that TV movie would kill me, it's just too complicated this New York world of telephones and appointments. So I'll see you when I come to NY again with galleys, next week. I have angle for piano here now so dont worry about piano. Jerry Wald I think wants me to try a screen original for him but I wonder if I really would know how—Anyway I STILL havent got going on Memory Babe? See what I mean? I should have got a home in Virginia or someplace. —On top of that George and Mona* trying to get me to meet thousands of girls around here,† that would really be the end of my memory babe work so I refused.— I'm working on Memory babe right now this weekend. See you soon.

Jack

■

There was a distinct change in voice in the letters Jack was sending me now. He was writing in a different rhythm in short, dead, angry sentences like the dry rat-tat-tat of a drum. The text bristled with periods rather than the dashes that had punctuated his flow of language before.

As Jack struggled with *Memory Babe*, a novel he would abandon by the end of the summer, his writing was bringing him no "ecstasy of mind"; in fact, it only served to accelerate his drinking. I had noticed on my visit to Northport that he was consuming hard liquor now that he could afford it, rather than cheap wine, and that his mother, while she deplored the state Jack was in, drank right along with him.

---

*Jack's Northport neighbors.
†"I have a slew of girls in NY now," Jack wrote to Philip Whalen on June 12, "and screwing them all and wish Gary was here to help, just too many. One night I was in bed with 3 girls. I'm getting too old for this. I try to serve the Bodhisattva's role for them but this ole Bodhisattva's getting tired."

In his journal four years later, in a rare moment of excruciating, absolutely sober self-knowledge, Jack would own up to the effect alcohol had upon the way he wrote:

"I dont write anything but fat short outcries by hand. I dont write anything but insulting letters. . . .

"I cant think of the right word (Aphasia) nor remember what I did when I was drunk (Amnesia), just a horrifying guiltiness that I've destroyed & befouled everything again."

June 16, 1958

Dear Jack,

How nice to find a letter from you—even though filled with anger (justifiable) at Viking, N.Y., phones, etc. Sure, I'll forward your letter to Hiram tonight—although I'm too bugged about my own book to write to him about that, and I'll also send you the letter from Bob Lax. Leon and Joan, incidentally, went away to the country last week, which was why you couldn't get in touch with him, but he'll be back this week. (Why didn't you get in touch with me while you were at it, Rat?)

Listen, Memory Babe, yes I want to see you when you come in and hope you'll stay overnight and we'll make love and all that jazz . . . BUT please try to call me before you come (you can even call me from Northport the night before—35 cents ain't much for a rich novelist)—or call me at the office (OR 5 2010) when you get into town (but not between 12:30 and 1:45 when I'm out to lunch)—you know my last name, just ask for Miss Glassman. This may look complicated, but isn't really—so, like, please do try. I don't exactly live in a vacuum here, you know. And it's awful expecting you all week (like last week) and not even hearing from you that you can't see me. That's just not kind. Ah, but I do want to see you—I really miss you like crazy sometimes, especially these soft summer nights—and I suppose you'll forget to call and come banging in here at 4 AM when the last bar is closed, demanding eggs, and I'll be mad at you for about two seconds—I can't stay mad at you somehow. . . . But even so, *try!*

I'm glad you've started on the new book—it sounded to me that that was going to be the most beautiful of them all. But you must try to ride on top of this whole N.Y. scene instead of letting it ride you, and that goes for the Northport scene too. I think—if you'll pardon me—that you tend to let things build up inside your mind until they become far more menacing than they really are—like you're writing some kind of surrealistic novel about the destruction of Baron Jean Louis Kerouac, in which the castle burns down and men with swords come and the plague is in the next town. My God! you don't have to do anything you don't want to—you even have enough money now. In Virginia, you'd have Virginians or something. You have a home at last—so, relax in it—you know, if you go tiptoeing around and whispering all the time and jumping every time the door creaks or a car passes, you can give yourself a pretty bad scare. I'm not laughing at you, dear—I know you feel invaded and kind of naked, but half of that comes from inside of you. Stand still for a while and don't run. Things are worse when you run from them. You've made a place for yourself in the world, and there are great things about it and also annoyances, but then there are the annoyances of being obscure and broke. C'est la vie!

One thing—to bring up a dull subject—if you had a wife who was somewhat worldly, she might act as a kind of buffer for you (wives of writers often do that); if she loved you, she'd certainly let you take to the woods whenever you wanted to; she might also like being left alone now and then herself. Women are really just as great and as human as men, although different . . . I think of this now because there is a great chorus of little children in the courtyard now playing house, saying:

> your   your
> say   prayers   say   prayers   SAY YOUR PRAYERS

Who's my kid? You're my kid. No, I'm your husband. No, he is.

Well, I'm probably bugging you now with all my noise in the great ear of the void—so I'll stop. You come see me and buy me a big Chinese dinner. I have lots of gossip, but it will keep a few more days—too dull to write it all down.

A hundred hugs and thirty little kisses,
from
Brigitte Bardot
Francoise Sagan
All the Northport Heiresses
Sneakers the Cat
and
Jerce

■

When I wrote to Jack now, I was increasingly careful not to reveal my hurt feelings. I would write draft after draft and tear them up, finally arriving at a version that seemed safe enough to send him. In this case, I'd made the mistake of letting down my guard by bringing up the subject of marriage—though undoubtedly I'd convinced myself that I was doing it in the coolest hypothetical way.

Did I really want to marry Jack now that the situation seemed more hopeless than ever?

I'd grown up believing the widely held fallacy that love could conquer all, and it would be a long time before I could let go of it, despite evidence to the contrary. I was Beat, but I was also a woman of the 1950s, when marrying the man one loved was the all-important goal. It was harder than I'd thought to live alone. Somehow Jack's new house made me feel orphaned.

For all my experience, of course, I was still naively, dangerously romantic. By now I had a sense of what marriage to Jack would be like, and I'd always known that if it happened, it would probably not be permanent. Even so, I would have married him if he'd asked me—despite Mcmere, despite his drinking—and tried to hang on. Wasn't that how you proved yourself—by taking on a difficult love and enduring somehow? If you were a woman, wasn't your "road" the man you gave yourself to?

■

Hey Baby, where you at?

A letter from Allen has arrived—shall I forward it or will you be coming in shortly?

Haven't negotiated Proust yet—too hot, feet hurt, etc.—but will this week sometime. But I've gone and lost that piece of paper with the other book you wanted. Will you tell it to me again?

What are you doing? Are you finally working full steam on MEMORY BABE?

Lots of distracting new people in New York—a younger generation of Jacks and Allens—very gentle adventurers all about to take off for the Orient, Mexico, mountains, the sea, the moon perhaps. You would like them and should meet them. They wouldn't tire you. What a sense of possibility they have. They make me feel aged. I find myself putting them down a bit just out of jealousy or something, and feel sad about that.

Robert sends regards. He'd like to drive out one day and see you, maybe bringing me with him unless you'd consider that too horrible to bear. So if you see old beat car one day, don't be too surprised that it's city types and not Northport bathing beauties. How are those little girls, by the way? Don't let them Dylan Thomas you, however charmingly—all young kids want their heroes martyred, being madly and coldly desirous of a feeling of significance (usually significant destruction, I'm afraid). Yes, me too, not so long ago.

Sweetie, I hope you come in soon. I do want to talk to you. Maybe we can make Lucien a six-inch steak and we can all lie on the rug and listen to jazz—Elise has brought down her phonograph which works very well, even though she's hardly ever home anymore, since she's found one of these young adventurers to make it with. Well . . . you've still got your key. Don't feel guilty about using it. Okay?

Regards to your mother.

Love,

Joyce

■

In the spring, Elise had unexpectedly returned from San Francisco. She hadn't written me for months or even sent me her address. She was very thin and quiet. She showed me the long scar on her belly from a late-term abortion by cesarean section; it had taken Elise too long to find a psychiatrist willing to certify that she would kill herself if she had to have a baby. She had little to say about her adventures in North Beach.

At first Elise stayed with her parents in Washington Heights, waiting for Allen Ginsberg to come back from Paris. In June I invited her to move in with me. We kept each other company, roaming the Village and the Lower East Side at all hours, meeting new people. Still in love with Allen, she understood that I could not bring myself to break up with Jack quite yet, that I could only disengage myself when our relationship hit bottom. But she predicted that I would never regret loving Jack.

When Allen had returned in May, Elise had realized there was little room for her in his life. He had come back to join Peter Orlovsky, and they seemed as "married" in their East Second Street walkup as any heterosexual couple.

On the phonograph Elise had brought down to my apartment, we played my Billie Holiday records over and over again. "I'm through with love," Billie sang, though you knew she didn't mean it. But I was learning that love changed when hope went out of it.

■

August 14, 1958

Dear Joyce— Thought of a great title for your book—Pay Me the Penny After (a line from Memory Babe)— Still looking forward to seeing you this Fall—Memory B. 1/3rd done— Feel very happy that I have no commitments to see *anybody*— That's the point— Another title I saw on an insurance form: LOSS PAYABLE TO, but the first one is really classic— I still no receive money from Hollywood! I guess they figure I'm too beat to deserve payment.

Jean Louis

Thursday

Dear Jack,

Your card made me so happy. I've missed your voice, you know. I've wanted to write you all week, but felt too shy somehow. But now it's ten in the morning and Lester Young is playing sweetly on the phonograph and the cats are drowsing with their heads in the dustpan—and I don't feel shy. If you were here, I'd make us a pot of coffee—but, no, I guess if you were here, you'd be sleeping and so would I, and the cats would be asleep on our stomachs because they are stomach cats. However, here I am at my typewriter. If I sound jobless again, it's because I've taken off this week to work on the novel.

Hey, I did like "Pay me the penny after"*—I like the sound it has. But the novel's such a hung-up, nervous thing right now. It's difficult for me to think of it ever being finished and needing a title to carry it into the world. I *am* going to finish it though, but it's going to be blood all the way. I shall never take such a long time writing anything again. Baby, I'm not going to bore you by enumerating all my novelistic woes. I am keeping calm on Dexamil, have rented this typewriter which jumps, dammit, and have

---

*Jack's variation on "Fly now, pay later."

bought six dollars worth of paper upon which I will hopefully type it up. Oh, every time I read my own prose lately, I could die from shame and disappointment. But somehow writing it is fine even if reading it is not fine and thinking about it is terrible. This is a happy week. I feel claustrophobic and manic and never know what time it is and there is always the same blue light in this apartment and sometimes what I've just written surprises me. In the evening, big parties of people pass through this apartment leaving ashes and copies of Yugen and unfinished cups of jasmine tea and wine jugs—it is usually Howard Schulman, who is going to the Coast on Saturday, and endlessly saying goodbye to Elise and me. Diane di Prima comes in white slacks and dances with Howard to Fats Domino "Goodbye Fat Man" music. Howard dances knee-in-groin style, but is picking up on a new style now which is the "I-don't-give-a-shit-for-you-Baby" style, to be done with slick hair and long cool body in a red shirt and an unremovable cigarette—while the girl knocks herself out. Howard is intent upon becoming "the angel-headed hipster" of all time and showing those West Coast Cats a thing or two. What will become of him, I don't know—nothing bad, I hope. Leo Garen comes and plays the cornet with such astounding sweetness, so you remember that he is really wistful orphaned Leo after all and not just Leo G. teahead shark. Well, all these people say to me, "Write your novel, Man," and I say, "Yes, that's what I'm going to do," and wake up alone in the morning glad that no one's dancing in the living room except the cats. If you were dancing in the living room, it would be different, because no matter what you do you carry great silence with you.

I guess by the time you come in, New York will have quieted down, and you mustn't let it clamour at you the way it did last year. You'd be heartened to see how quietly and freely Allen moves through the city. You can do that too, Sweetie, if you want. Allen tells me that Gary [Snyder] and Phil Whalen are coming in, so I'll bet you'll have a beautiful Fall. Everyone loves you and will stand with you. You won't be alone in the angry literary jungle like you were last year—I often wished then that

Allen were here for your sake. I remember the first party we went to last Fall. You said, "Protect me," and I wanted to with all my heart, but didn't do a very good job, having all my own old shynesses and especially my strange shyness of you—it was always like maybe you were going off in a taxi any minute and I'd never see you again, and had we ever known each other after all? . . .

I'm so glad MEMORY BABE is finally swinging along—is it as you told me once divided into sections which are the houses you lived in, and is its prose like OCTOBER IN THE RAIL-ROAD EARTH? Are you feeling better now, Baby? Has your hand stopped hurting? I do worry about you.

Well . . . I hope Fall comes early this year. Until then—

Love,
Joyce

Je te baise mille fois et les petits chats te baise aussi. Write if you feel like it. I'll write you again.

[Northport, Long Island]
[mid-August]

Dear Joyce

Your prose is probably not as bad as you think, especially if you let your "hateful" first drafts rest a week or two before you edit them (which you shouldnt do at all). But if you feel such remorse about yr prose somehow that sounds good to me, as if you were really doing good. Your trouble is probably the same I'm having with Memory Babe, boredom with the story. Memory Babe events are so far back I dont remember any details any more and the details are the life of any story. However I just lackadaisically wrote several thousand words on the roll and re-read them and they get better with every reading. It's like, on tea for instance, you think you're a blazing genius while writing and then afterwards it's really not as good. So that if you write with excruciating shame, it's probably bound to be real good. But now that I know all these really true inner secrets of writing I'VE LOST ALL INTEREST IN LITERATURE dammit, I just dont

158

care to write & describe anything. To give Memory Babe form, for instance, I piled up a series of typical events on a Xmas weekend in Lowell 1933, packed tight with events but the details really elude me almost. In the middle of Memory Babe, as its sourceful flower, is The Heavenly Vision of Memory Babe, that being a vision of the Manger experience by lil Ti Jean me. As I stare at the golden eternity in the crib everything disappears except the golden eternity. Prior to that I'm a shepherd boy, with my Lowell chums, and the 3 wise kings turn out to be the town drunk, the town swearer, and the town sadman. Sad, not mad. St. Joseph appears to be my father but the Virgin is unidentifiable. St. Joseph is also Buddha. My sister carries buckets at the inn. I am an idiot, or that is, an imbecile shepherd boy. When I wake up Xmas morning it's like Scrooge, I do all the things I should have, like church, like dragging my father to see his sad brother, all the details of the town previous to the vision. This is the best possible form for BABE, I contemplated it for months and months even a year you know, but now that I have the form I feel uninterested. Yet as I say it seems to be good when I look at it, Dharma Bums was the same drag. O yes, the prose I keep simple, like in Dharma Bums, that is, halfway between On the Road prose and the prose of Railroad earth* . . . actually Railroad earth prose is too tough to deliver the message I wanta deliver to ordinary people. There is a certain value in simplicity too, in communicating to everybody on all levels, but that bores me because I'm such an arty shit.

I got a nice letter from Allen, will go see him in his new pad again, he sternly warns me not to show up drunk, says the pad is a quiet castle for thought. Is Leo really good? that would be strange if he became a professional cornetist. He may be born for it, he does remind me of Gershwin, musician-like face. I've been nice & quiet here, bought all the furniture finally, round table in kitchen (new maple solid) and got everything but desk and tape recorder and painting kits. I do have a beautiful AmFm Zenith

*"October in the Railroad Earth," a prose piece about Jack's day as a railroad brakeman.

159

radio that plays big Matthew Passions all day with a big round tone ($60 radio). and I got a tremendous $85 Webcor 4 speed that plays my poems and albums booming deep. But I'm not happy, I can see now I'll have to be getting that shack in the north woods soon and go to it once in a while, to recuperate from world, which enters my house via TV, driveway, staring neighbors, George Eddy's stream of gals who just about come in and grab my cock but I dont want to get in trouble around here or get caught up in their hysterical whirls, boy, do they party around here! People around here are worse than the Beat generation. Drunk, crazy. Yes, my hand stopt hurting when I discovered the trouble was in the wrist and treated it there. My mother is very happy now that my friends dont visit me,—gave her the house and she enjoys her privacy in it. I'll see my friends myself when I go out. Thats better. Also my house is my office for work. Sounds like it will be a whacky Fall with Snyder and Whalen, wow. Allen says he wants all of us to give big free poetry reading to multitudes he says, not me. I can listen. I had an invitation to be on a forum with Max Lerner about Beats, for $100 honorarium, Brandeis Univ. I dont want to be sneered at by no liberals in public. But I will go to Canada for Holiday in October. MGM is putting out a movie called Beat Gen. without even having consulted me about my 1955 copyright of that title, under name Jean-Louis, so my lawyer will fight, meanwhile On the Road people broke, sent me nothing, it's a mess, and Subterraneans at MGM waiting for okay of lawyer in beret. So, so far, $2000 from millionaire hollywood is what I got.

Jack

Oh yes, and Chicago Review wanted me to write a commentary on a silly interview Norman Mailer had with somebody, concerning "Hip" and "God" in which Mailer says God is an embattled being fighting in the universe, Manichaeanism, which is not my idea of the golden eternity God of nothing-ever-happens-anyway including good and evil, light and darkness. But, too, his concern suddenly with Hip is very square and bandwagony. I wonder what

Allen would have said to read it . . . tho Mailer did say some striking things when he stuck to his own mind's interests (socialistic, atheism, etc.) because he says God is dying which is ridiculous. Anyway phooey on commentaries anyway. And I dont want personal involvement with Mailer or any writers but my own boys . . . and not even them, really. My cats Timmy & Tyke are fine, gentle little beings enduring time with me . . . and my mother is happy and grateful and plays around her house I mean like a child with a new toy house (decorations, etc.) She told me I was all set and well protected now, by her special prayers, so I got nothin to worry about except my own giddiness and gripes. Funny, the nuns and Dorothy King also say special prayers for me and assure me I'm all set now. But I believe them. Imagine what Mailer would say!

Joyce, when I come into NY this Fall I hope you wont get mad at me if I fiddle around with other girlfriends a little, I dont wanta be "Steadies" with anybody, now if this hurts you why?— does Allen get mad when I go visit Joe Blow instead of him? Don't OWN me, just be my nice little blonde friend and dont be sad because I'm a confirmed bachelor & hermit. Hard to talk about this, I guess you're sore all over again. Well, if I do fiddle around with other girls, which is really unlikely in a way, you wont know about it. For instance, Robt. says he saw you with another boy in the park and it made me GLAD for you, not jealous. So remember. In fact your salvation is within yourself, in your own essence of mind, it is not to be gotten grasping at external people like me. You know it too, Buddha.

JeanLouis

PS At last I get Symphony Sid *all night* on 97.9 FM! What a magic twist! Because I was too far from AM New York.

PS—I decided to do that Lerner talk, money for oil paints & vitamins (Nov. 7)

PPSS—I think I'll start Memory Babe all over again, no dexamyl

Dear Jack,

Well, Sweetie, about your last paragraph—all I have to say, really, is that it will be lovely to see you again, and that I mean with all my heart. If you walked in this moment, I would leap up and kiss you, even if you hadn't shaved for two weeks. And no, I don't want to "own" you (that was never what I wanted)—but if we come together when we both want to do that and we truly swing, then that's okay, isn't it? (And I don't mean it has to be fun, fun, fun all the time—I love you equally when you're bugged.) But just one word of warning—I am *not* Allen Ginsberg! I think he's terrific in his way, but we're different. And you must learn to be more of a Frenchman and say "Vive la difference!" Also, if you have secrets—please do try to keep them. So . . . like, the door's still the same door, and you have the same key. . . .

You were absolutely right about my novel boredom, but my dexamyl highs have helped me work up interest again, thank God!, and Haydn's giving me an extension, says "Take as long as you want," but I'm going to finish very soon and begin Novel II.

And please don't *you* get disinterested in literature! I like the Xmas weekend idea. You haven't really started all over again, have you? And where did you get the idea that you were an "arty shit"? Ridiculous! I read the Dharma Bums selection in the Chicago Review and thought it very beautiful. I think the dopey Northport people are giving you a depressing opinion of yourself. Come to NY and let Allen scream at you—except that he doesn't scream anymore, but is all gentle now and quietly wise—he makes me feel terribly frivolous.

I've been wanting to write this all week. I sometimes get hung-up about answering letters. I've been kind of disoriented for awhile. Elise, who was living here all summer, suddenly last Tuesday up and absconded to San Francisco with young beautiful boy Keith in a speeding car driven by Howard Schulman. And it's always hard for me to get used to people suddenly being absent. There's something sad and disconcerting about the eternal stability of furniture and objects when someone's gone. Elise, especially, who I probably won't see again for years—I feel as though someone took a pencil and drew a black line across my life. She was sitting on the couch going through her old letters and papers and throwing things out and putting things away, and I realized that we had both grown up, which was great and awful at the same time. It's funny, but after all the years of knowing each other, this summer we really got to know each other well—with so many old images tossed out at last. I could never write that poem I wrote about her now. I'm awfully happy for her—she loves and is loved and everything is blooming for her; she has put away all her black dresses and wears orange. And the thing with Keith is good—they have adventures together just walking down the block. Too bad you didn't get to meet him—he's quiet and clear-seeing and incredibly and beautifully American, he looks a bit like Lucien—has a funny, blond lopsided mustache and little-boy face—his father was a printer, like yours . . . I think Allen was sad when Elise left . . .

Well, dexamyl pill has taken effect . . . and I'd better start on the novel now . . .

Give my regards to your mother. I'm glad she's happy in that old brown house.

Luv,
yer dexed-up frend,
Jerce

P.S. Have terrific working phonograph now—Elise left me hers. Also new Bird and Billie Holiday records, and Lester Young. When winter comes, I'll buy me some Bach.

P.S. Bought jasmine tea in Chinatown. There is always exactly one flower and one little twig in each cup.

Part VI

.

September-November,

1958

J ACK HAD PROMISED he'd come back in the fall, and he did. Though I didn't bring the subject up, I was painfully aware he had made a number of trips to the city during the summer without seeing me. He never explained his aloofness, he just reappeared in my life, coming in for long, chaotic weekends of endless drinking with his friends, returning to Memere on the Long Island Railroad, gray-faced and exhausted.

I remember that we saw a lot of Allen Ginsberg and Peter Orlovsky and that on one occasion Allen had me telephone his old Columbia classmate, the critic Norman Podhoretz, who had been attacking the Beat writers, and invite Podhoretz over for tea with Jack and Allen at Lucien's apartment, the most respectable venue he could think of. Podhoretz showed up, but there was no rapprochement. He was huffily offended when Jack and Allen offered him marijuana. The tea party ended with Jack profoundly depressed and Allen shouting angrily at Podhoretz, "We'll get your children!"

Jack and I also frequently visited Robert and Mary Frank in their loft on the Bowery, where there was much excited talk as we sat around their big oak table—exactly the kind of table Jack wanted for his mother's kitchen—of the movie Robert was planning to make in the spring, based on Jack's play. Mary was a gifted sculptor, only a few years older than I was. She was the first dedicated woman artist I had ever met, obviously torn between the desire to throw herself into her work and the demands of taking care of her husband and two small children. She and her close friend Dodie Muller, whose husband, the painter Jan Muller, had died the previous year, wore flamboyant outfits that impressed me greatly—put together from 1920s clothes they found in thrift shops. They called themselves the Beat Pre-Raphaelites. Dodie was a dark-haired woman from Texas, a direct descendant of Jesse James and part American Indian like Jack; at the parties we went to she was one of the wildest dancers. It was obvious that she'd been desperately lonely since her husband's death, and it did not escape me that she and Jack were attracted to one another.

One day that fall when I was visiting him during one of Jack's absences, Allen Ginsberg said to me, "You should be patient and stay with Jack. He'll always have other women, but he'll always come home and tell you all about it."

I said, "But I can't live that way, Allen."

And I knew I'd spoken the truth.

■

Oct. 7

LiPo Babe,

Here's a nice review from the World-Telegram today—ol' octagon Hanscom* ain't so octagonal after all, maybe.

Allen tells me you were blue when you got home, because of slit-eyed, well-dressed people.† UGH! The Hell with them! They're not even alive really. Dig them and walk away.

---

*Leslie Hanscom had reviewed *Dharma Bums*. He had also been the first reporter to interview Jack following the publication of *On the Road*.

†Jack had come into New York for the publication party for *The Dharma Bums*, after which he wrote Allen, "Like America I'm getting a nervous breakdown. . . . All these well dressed people looking at me with slitted eyes, why don't I just retire from the universe—Ah fuck it, I'm going back to Li Po—I hate my beating heart—Something's wrong with the world. . . . Grandfather Night in this old house scares me with its black coffin."

Love meanwhile,
Kisses,
Ecstasy pie,
ice cream (vanilla).
Chinese poems,
mountains,
cats,
Symphony Sid,—

all for you!
Jerce

October 16

Dear Jack,

Here are two reviews, Sweetie. One, the Dallas guy, really swings, n'est-ce pas? The other don't know what he talking about and comes on very strangely. Showed these to Allen, whom I also lent long review by V. S. Pritchett in the London New Statesman Literary Supplement, which praises you lots, compares you to Huck Finn (at last!). You'll see it as soon as I get it back and send it. But it does look as though the air's finally beginning to clear for you. Imagine how they'll flip over DR. SAX! Enclosed is also angry letter by me (in best impersonal, stuffy style because it does no good if they say "Aw, she's his girl, or something.") to Saturday Review, which—shit! I don't have it with me, but it's incredibly stupid and awful and makes the reviewer look like an envious ass actually.

How are you? Allen and Lucien have told me about the mad weekend. Thought maybe I'd see you either coming into or leaving NY. I was incarcerated with BREAKING WINDOWS over 3-day weekend (because of Columbus Day), writing and making borscht and beef stew, which I'm still eating.

Long letter from Howard Schulman, enclosing short one to you, which I'll send. Write him if you can—he's lonesome out there, having a rough time with the cops—San Francisco sounds pretty sinister to me, just like you described it last summer.

169

Made bar-tour with Allen and Peter last night and met their Paris friend B.J.—very handsome, sweet guy with charming French wife whom you would dig (brunette) and who keeps saying with French accent, "Eet's a gahss." You will like B.J. too, I think. Everyone everywhere rushes up to Allen and says, Will you explain this image of lobotomy in HOWL etc., will you read poetry for hundreds of dollars?—you know the scene—very wearing. If you come this week, there'll still be borscht, if that's an inducement. I had a dream about you—your mother going off in a snowstorm to look for you, while everyone sat around in your garden to wait for you where it was summer.

Love,
Joyce

[late October]
Saturday,

Hello Elise,

Saturday morning on the East Side—sun and very red peppers, the first pomegranates, and evil purple cauliflowers . . . How you? You sounded great on phone—sweet and peaceful, no more raggedness in your voice. The cats scrambling upon my lap now, would no doubt send you their feline love too if they weren't thinking about sardines and roaches and the sad disappearance of the garbage . . . Well, the apartment is coated nicely with ashes and bottles and dried up beer puddles, sex stains on sheets, torn poems and what have you— Jack left last night after a whole week (!) in NY,* and I am a little hung-over, a little sleepy, a little high on conversation. Happy. Twenty-three years old. My teeth are floating in my mouth a bit, but that's okay. I will clean soon, but not yet. Like to contemplate this friendly mess. Hey, the book is now entitled: BREAKING WINDOWS (Jack, Allen, Joan P., and I all like that—do you?), and the window has actually been broken with a few too many adverbs

*Memere had gone to Orlando for a month to visit her daughter.

and "suddenly"s perhaps, but they'll come out with a stroke of the pencil. I bought lots of soup and will stay in house all weekend. Cut two days of work this week and wish I could cut it altogether.

Write and tell me all about your Berkeley pad—have you got a rented tree? Elise, I haven't been able to make it up to your bank this week, but will next, honest. Leo Skir calls and asks about you, desires a postcard or something. Allen asks after you. . . . Allen's beginning to rush around a lot, trying to get everybody published, and is starting to worry about doing too much of that, wonders how he can make some money—he doesn't really feel like writing articles . . . Ah, but he's bringing Jack to life again—Jack said yesterday he loves Allen more than he ever did before, and talks about giving up Northport house, dumping mother in Florida (admits she inhibits him) and living in NY, with sometime shack in woods to retreat to now and then and jeepster. Maybe that's the way for him to live, I don't know—but he's really not feeling well at all, is always going to sleep on the floor now, no matter where. Allen thinks it would be a good idea for Jack to marry me, though he laughs and says, "Of course he wouldn't be a very good catch . . ." Oh, it's turning out to be endless. What should I do? What can I do? No answers, are there? Funny how happiness can be just lugging a sweet, groggy drunk home in a taxi. Acceptance, I guess, is the answer, and *Salve los ninos!*, with the chips falling wherever they fall. In another twenty years, the next Ice Age will officially begin (true—see October Harper's) ushered in by tidal waves, the evacuation of Brooklyn, levees around NY, and then the descent of the glaciers—all televised. The scientists are all delighted with this theory: "The recent epoch (11,000 years) may be considered as just another interglacial period." —which puts us, bomb and all, nicely in our places, and makes everything relative, senseless, and completely useless somehow.

Aint you glad, Babe?

Love,
Jerce

I t wasn't going to be endless. The weekend after I wrote Elise, my relationship with Jack ended abruptly in front of an Italian restaurant in the Village, where we had gone with Robert and Mary Frank and a group of artists. Dodie Muller was sitting next to Jack at the table. Right in front of me, Jack started flirting outrageously with Dodie, and she was clearly ready to tumble into bed with him. I couldn't bear it. It would never work out with Jack, it would only get more painful. I pushed back my chair and stood up and insisted he come outside with me.

"You're nothing but a big bag of wind," I shouted when we were out in the street, which wasn't what I'd intended to say at all.

Jack blathered something about "noblesse oblige" and "Unrequited love's a bore" (a Cole Porter line that would soon crop up again in his narration for the film *Pull My Daisy*), and I rushed away from him. Just once I looked back to see if he was still standing where I'd left him, but he was gone.

In 1962, Jack gave Hiram Haydn an extravagant blurb for the publication of my novel *Come and Join the Dance*: "The best woman writer in America." I wanted to know what he'd really thought, but didn't try to write Jack, doubting he wanted to hear from me.

Shortly after my novel came out, my mother called about an item she'd just seen in the *World Telegram:* WOMAN, 28, FOUND DEAD. The nameless woman was Elise Cowen. For the past year or so I'd rarely seen her. Unable to give up her love for Allen, she had left her boyfriend Keith in 1960 and returned to New York. When Allen and Peter sailed off for a long stay in India in the spring of 1961, Elise went adrift in the streets of the East Village—going where I could not follow into the underworld of drugs, carrying her secret notebooks of poems in a shopping bag from pad to pad. One night she turned up at my door to borrow a typewriter, her face withered by methedrine. Soon after that, I heard that her parents had put her into a mental hospital. In February, after being released into their custody, she jumped from their living-room widow. For a long time I was haunted by something Elise said to me the summer we lived together: "I wonder how I'll wear my hair when I'm thirty."

In my own way, I too had been adrift, spending too much time at the Cedar Tavern, going home with too many different men, as if you could stumble upon a shortcut to love. In March, a stranger appeared in the Cedar. We'd noticed each other a few nights earlier at a party, where, as we watched others doing that new dance the Twist, he had asked me a searching and memorable question— "Why do you hang back?"—then abruptly disappeared. His name was James Johnson. He bought me a glass of wine, after which we went for a long walk all the way down to Chinatown and back, telling each other our lives.

It was only a week since Jim had left his car keys and his bankbook on a kitchen table in Lake Erie, Ohio, and boarded a bus at the Greyhound terminal in Cleveland. He had come to New York to paint, to breathe, leaving behind him a cold marriage, a couple of kids he thought about with anguish, and a job teaching art to debutantes. He said he knew he had to change everything or die. Since Elise's death, I had been feeling the same way about myself. I told him he could take over my apartment if he needed one, since I was planning to go to Rome. It took us one night to know we wanted to be with each other for good.

In the fall of 1963, unaware of my recent marriage to Jim, Jack called me out of the blue, perhaps in the hope of starting again or just for old time's sake. Maybe he was thinking of me because he'd recently been working on *Desolation Angels*. Who knew? "Come over to Lucien's house," he said. "Bring your little husband." Jim reluctantly agreed to come with me. Jack was drunk by the time we got there—a raging kind of drunkenness I'd never seen in the past. His beautiful face was red and bloated. When a loud argument broke out between Jack and Lucien and they started jabbing at each other with their lighted cigarettes, we left.

My husband was a drinker who was desperately trying to stop. He was killed in a motorcycle accident that December. A couple of months later, I got a phone call from Jack—one of those late-night phone calls he had begun making to friends from the seclusion of the latest house he shared with his mother. They had moved several times, often at the instigation of Memere, who seemed to be as unsatisfiable and as homeless in her soul as her son, zigzagging between houses in Northport and Orlando and using up whatever money Jack made in the process. By now they were living in Northport for the third time while Jack looked for real estate in New England.

I tried to talk about what had happened to Jim, but Jack didn't seem to hear me. "You never wanted furs," he said. "All you ever wanted was a little pea soup." I didn't tell him I had wanted and needed much more from him than that, and that I'd finally found it with the husband I'd just lost.

In 1965 I read Jack's description of me in *Desolation Angels*: "an interesting young person, a Jewess, elegant, middleclass sad and looking for something."

He surprised me and touched me by saying it was "perhaps the best love affair I ever had."

"In fact she sorta fell in love with me," Jack wrote. "But that was only because I didn't impose on her."

Index

DATE DUE

SEP 1 5 2000	
NOV 1 6 2000	
MAR 1 4 2001	
APR 2 0 2001	
MAY 1 6 2001	
AUG 0 5 2003	
JUN 0 1 2010	
JUN 3 0 2014	

GAYLORD   PRINTED IN U.S.A.